PEN
LAN

Ruskin Bond's first novel, *The Room on the Roof*, written when he was seventeen, won the John Llewellyn Rhys Memorial Prize in 1957. Since then he has written several novellas (including *Vagrants in the Valley*, *A Flight of Pigeons* and *Delhi Is Not Far*), essays, poems and children's books, many of which have been published by Penguin India. He has also written over 500 short stories and articles that have appeared in a number of magazines and anthologies. He received a Sahitya Akademi Award in 1993, and the Padma Shri in 1999.

Ruskin Bond was born in Kasauli, Himachal Pradesh, and grew up in Jamnagar, Dehradun, Delhi and Simla. As a young man, he spent four years in the Channel Islands and London. He returned to India in 1955, and has never left the country since. He now lives in Landour, Mussoorie, with his extended family.

ALSO BY RUSKIN BOND

Fiction
The Night Train at Deoli and Other Stories
Time Stops at Shamli and Other Stories
The Room on the Roof and Vagrants in the Valley
Our Trees Still Grow in Dehra
Delhi Is Not Far
Collected Fiction (1956-1996)
Strangers in the Night: Two Novellas
Season of Ghosts
Friends in Small Places
When Darkness Falls and Other Stories
A Flight of Pigeons

Non-fiction
Rain in the Mountains
Scenes from a Writer's Life
The Lamp Is Lit
The Little Book of Comfort

Anthologies (edited)
The Penguin Book of Indian Ghost Stories
The Penguin Book of Indian Railway Stories
The Penguin Book of Indian Classical Love Stories and Lyrics

Puffin
Treasury of Stories for Children
Panther's Moon and Other Stories
The Room on the Roof

Landour Days

A Writer's Journal

Ruskin Bond

PENGUIN BOOKS

PENGUIN BOOKS
Published by the Penguin Group
Penguin Books India Pvt. Ltd, 11 Community Centre, Panchsheel Park, New Delhi 110 017, India
Penguin Group (USA) Inc., 375 Hudson Street, New York, New York 10014, USA
Penguin Group (Canada), 90 Eglinton Avenue East, Suite 700, Toronto, Ontario, M4P 2Y3, Canada (a division of Pearson Penguin Canada Inc.)
Penguin Books Ltd, 80 Strand, London WC2R 0RL, England
Penguin Ireland, 25 St Stephen's Green, Dublin 2, Ireland (a division of Penguin Books Ltd)
Penguin Group (Australia), 250 Camberwell Road, Camberwell, Victoria 3124, Australia (a division of Pearson Australia Group Pty Ltd)
Penguin Group (NZ), cnr Airborne and Rosedale Roads, Albany, Auckland 1310, New Zealand (a division of Pearson New Zealand Ltd)
Penguin Group (South Africa) (Pty) Ltd, 24 Sturdee Avenue, Rosebank, Johannesburg 2196, South Africa

Penguin Books Ltd, Registered Offices: 80 Strand, London WC2R 0RL, England

First published in Viking by Penguin Books India 2002

Copyright © Ruskin Bond 2002

All rights reserved

10 9 8 7 6 5 4 3 2

Inside illustrations by Ajanta Guhathakurta

Typeset in *PalmSprings* by SÜRYA, New Delhi
Printed at Chaman Offset Printers, New Delhi

This book is sold subject to the condition that it shall not, by way of trade or otherwise, be lent, resold, hired out, or otherwise circulated without the publisher's prior written consent in any form of binding or cover other than that in which it is published and without a similar condition including this condition being imposed on the subsequent purchaser and without limiting the rights under copyright reserved above, no part of this publication may be reproduced, stored in or introduced into a retrieval system, or transmitted in any form or by any means (electronic, mechanical, photocopying, recording or otherwise), without the prior written permission of both the copyright owner and the above-mentioned publisher of this book.

To the founder members of the Writers' Bar—Ganesh Saili, Nandu Jauhar, Vishal Ohri—in gratitude for keeping me in good spirits.

CONTENTS

Acknowledgements ... ix
Introduction ... xi

SUMMER ... 1

   April ... 3
   May ... 15
   June ... 31

MONSOON ... 49

   July ... 51
   August ... 62

AUTUMN   77

  September   79
  October   90

WINTER   101

  November   103
  December   113
  January   122
  February   126
  March   134

ACKNOWLEDGEMENTS

My thanks to Sayoni Basu and Ravi Singh for their invaluable editorial help, and to Ajanta Guhathakurta for her charming illustrations.

INTRODUCTION

The habit of keeping a diary has led me into trouble more than once. The first time this happened was when I was at boarding school. At some point in my journal I went into raptures over the comely shape and generous proportions of my Housemaster's wife. My class teacher discovered the diary in my desk, read parts of it, and marched me off to the Housemaster's study, where I received a caning. The Housemaster kept my diary, and I have a feeling that his wife read it and was secretly amused (and possibly flattered) by my account of her physical attractions. Anyway, she went out of her way to be nice to me, and even held my hot, sweaty hand for a while when school closed and it was time to say goodbye. The Housemaster was not so forthcoming.

People love dipping into other people's diaries, and there were one or two other occasions when my entries resulted in embarrassment or ill feeling. But I am a compulsive diarist, and it has been difficult to stop me from recording my impressions of people, places and incidents, as well as my own self-searching thoughts and emotions. In this way I have preserved much that would otherwise have been forgotten. Naturally there were events, trivial in retrospect, which are better forgotten; but it is salutary for me to flip through the pages of these old diaries and notebooks and see how stupid I was at the time, or how I coped with difficult situations. I have always been a great one for putting down 'words to live by', although I haven't been very good at living up to them.

These journal entries also provide a record of my progress (or lack of it) as a full-time writer, and may be useful to young writers who have set out on the same road. It's a long and difficult journey, and at times it is discouraging. Bookers and Nobels do not come to all of us. Most writers have to make do with modest advances and occasional 'cheques in the mail'. And sometimes the mail is slow in arriving! In spite of discouragement, dedicated writers carry on. Never despair, is their motto. And if you do, then work on in despair.

Introduction • xiii

But the journals are not just about the writing life. They are also about day-to-day living, my relationship with the world of nature (which in some ways has taken the place of religion), and with the people who live with me and around me.

These are only extracts, of course, from my journal of the last year or so. In the autumn of my life, I grow reflective, and so some of them are almost like essays. Some months I write often, sometimes I do not touch my journal for days on end. Not everything that happens around me goes into my diary. The privacy of friends has to be respected. My own privacy has to be preserved, to a certain extent. But I am a subjective writer, and much that I have written over the years has been drawn from personal experience.

A sense of humour will help you to get through the worst of times. A little light laughter is the best kind of magic. I hope some of it comes through in these pages.

Summer

APRIL

Swifts are busy nesting in the roof and performing acrobatics outside my window. They do everything on the wing, it seems including feeding and making love. Mating in mid-air must be quite a feat. It's not in the *Kamasutra*.

The wind in the pines and deodars hums and moans, but in the chestnut it rustles and chatters and makes cheerful conversation. The horse chestnut in full leaf is a magnificent sight.

~

Amongst the current fraternity of writers, I must be that very rare person, an author who actually writes by hand.

Soon after the invention of the typewriter, most

editors and publishers understandably refused to look at any manuscript that was handwritten. A few years earlier, when Dickens and Balzac had submitted their hefty manuscripts in longhand, no one had objected. Had their handwriting been awful, their manuscripts would still have been read. Fortunately for all concerned, these and other famous writers took pains over their handwriting.

Both Dickens and Thackeray had clear flourishing handwriting. Somerset Maugham had an upright, legible hand; Tagore, a fine flourish. Churchill's neat handwriting never wavered, even when he was under stress. I like the bold, clear, straightforward hand of Abraham Lincoln; it mirrors the man.

Not everyone had a beautiful hand. King Henry VIII had an untidy scrawl, but then, he was not a man of much refinement. Guy Fawkes, who tried to blow up the British Parliament, had a very shaky hand. With such a quiver, no wonder he failed in his attempt. Hitler's signature is ugly, as you might expect. And Napoleon's doesn't seem to know when to stop; how like the man!

When I think of the great eighteenth and nineteenth century writers, scratching away with their quill pens, filling hundreds of pages every month, I am amazed that their handwriting did not deteriorate into the sort of hieroglyphics that makes up the average doctor's prescription today. They knew how to write legibly, if only for the sake of the typesetters.

And it wasn't only authors who wrote with an elegant hand. Most of our parents and grandparents had distinctive styles of their own. I still have my father's last letter, written to me when I was at boarding school over sixty years ago. He used large, beautifully formed letters, and his thoughts seemed to have the same flow and clarity as his handwriting.

In his letter he advises nine-year-old Ruskin about his handwriting:

> I wanted to write before about your writing, Ruskin ... Sometimes I get letters from you in very small writing, as if you wanted to squeeze everything into one sheet of paper. It is not good for you or for your eyes, to get into the habit of writing so small ... Try and form a larger style of handwriting. Use more paper if necessary!

I did my best to follow his advice, and I'm glad to report that after a lifetime of penmanship, my handwriting is still readable.

Word processors and computers are the in thing now, and I do not object to these electronic aids any more than I objected to the mechanical aid of my old

Olympia typewriter, which is still going strong after forty years; the latter is at least impervious to power failures. Although I still do most of my writing in longhand, I follow the conventions by typing a second draft. But I would not enjoy my writing if I had to do it straight on to a machine. It isn't just the pleasure of writing by hand, although that's part of it. Sometimes I like taking my notebooks or writing pads to odd places. This particular entry is being composed on the steep hillside above the cottage in which I live. Part of the reason for sitting here is that there is a new postman on the route, and I don't want him to miss me. For a freelance writer, the postman is almost as important as

his publisher. He brings me editorial acceptances or rejections, the occasional cheques and sometimes a nice letter from a reader. I could, of course, sit here doing nothing, but as I have pencil and paper with me, and feel like using them, I shall write until the postman comes and maybe after he has gone, too.

Typewriters and computers were not designed with steep mountain slopes in mind. On one occasion last autumn I did carry my typewriter into the garden, and I am still trying to extricate a couple of acorns from under the keys, while the roller seems permanently stained from some fine yellow pollen dust from the deodar trees. But armed with pencils and paper, I can lie on the grass and write for hours. Provided there are a couple of cheese-and-tomato sandwiches within easy reach.

~

The smallest insect in the world is a sort of fairy fly and its body is only a fifth of a millimetre long. One can only just see it with the naked eye. Almost like a speck of dust, yet it has perfect little wings and little combs on its legs for preening itself.

That is perfection.

~

The nice thing about reaching a reasonable age (sixty plus) is that, along the way, one has collected a few pleasant memories. Life isn't always pleasant, but I find it's possible to shut out the darker recollections and dwell instead on life's happier moments. Psychiatrists may not agree with this method. They like their patients to unburden themselves and reveal their childhood traumas. But it's when we cannot escape our childhood traumas that we end up on the psychiatrist's couch.

Anyway, here's an example of being able to relive an old memory without regret:

Last week, after a gap of forty years, I climbed to the little temple of Sirkhanda Devi, a steep climb from the motor road at 8,000 feet to the summit at 10,000 feet. Forty years ago I'd walked the thirty-odd miles from Mussoorie to Kaddukhal; there was no motor road then, just a bridle path. Now buses and taxis bring tourists and pilgrims to Kaddukhal, but they still have to climb to the temple. Climbing is good for both body and soul.

The old bridle path has disappeared, but remnants of it can be seen in places. While climbing up from the new road, I came across a little cluster of huts and recognized the one in which I'd spent a night, before tramping on to Chamba. I was just a boy then ... Of course the old man who'd offered me hospitality was long gone, and his son had moved elsewhere, but there were children in the courtyard, and goats and chickens, and a tall deodar which had been no taller than me on that first visit. So here were memories flooding back in the nicest of ways.

To be perfectly honest, that night in the hut had not been so lovely, for the sheepskin rug on which I'd slept had been infested with vicious fleas and *khatmals*, and I'd stayed awake scratching into the early hours. But see how easy it is to put aside the less pleasant memory. Forget the bugs and think of the moon coming up over the mountains, and life becomes a little more tolerable.

Well, on this second occasion I entered the tiny temple on the hilltop and thanked the Devi for her blessings and told her that life had been good to me since I'd last been there.

I feel drawn to little temples on lonely hilltops. With the mist swirling round them, and the wind humming in the stunted pines, they absorb some of the magic and mystery of their surroundings and transmit it to the questing pilgrim.

Another memory revived when I accompanied the family to the sulphur springs outside Dehra, and discovered that this former wilderness had been turned into a little dhaba township, with the garbage left by tourists and picnickers littering the banks of the stream and being caught up on the rocks.

Here, fifty years ago, I bicycled with my friends, bathed, and rested in the shade of the ravine. Few people found their way there. Today, it has been 'developed' into a tourist spot, although there is no longer any sign of the hot spring that made it known in the first place. In shock, the spring appears to have gone underground.

All this is progress, of course, and I must confess to being sadly behind the times.

The other day a young Internet surfer asked me why I preferred using a pencil instead of a computer. The principal reason, I told him, was that I liked chewing on the end of my pencil. A nasty habit, but it helps me concentrate. And I find it extremely difficult to chew on a computer.

~

'We should not spoil what we have by desiring what we have not, but remember that what we have too was the gift of fortune'—Epicurus.

~

Glorious day. Walked up and around the hill, and got some of the cobwebs out of my head.

Some epigrams (my own, for future use):

A well-balanced person: someone with a chip on both shoulders.

Experience: The knowledge that enables you to recognize a mistake when you make it the second time.

Sympathy: What one woman offers another in exchange for details.

Worry: The interest paid on trouble before it becomes due.

I read these out to my critic and confidant, four-year-old Gautam (Siddharth's younger brother), and he shook his head sadly and responded with *'Kabi Khushi, Kabi Gam!'* Like Mr Dick in *David Copperfield*, he usually comes up with an appropriate response.

~

Death moves about at random, without discriminating between the innocent and the evil, the poor and the rich. The only difference is that the poor usually handle it better.

I heard today that the peanut vendor had died. The old man would always be in the dark, windy corner in Landour Bazaar, hunched up over the charcoal fire on which he roasted his peanuts. He'd been there for as long as I could remember, and he could be seen at almost any hour of the day or night. Summer or winter, he stayed close to his fire.

He was probably quite tall, but I never saw him standing up. One judged his height from his long, loose limbs. He was very thin, and the high cheekbones added to the tautness of his tightly stretched skin.

His peanuts were always fresh, crisp and hot. They were popular with the small boys who had a few coins to spend on their way to and from school, and with the patrons of the cinemas, many of whom made straight for the windy corner during intervals or when the show was over. On cold winter evenings, or misty monsoon days, there was always a demand for the old man's peanuts.

No one knew his name. No one had ever thought of asking him for it. One just took him for granted. He was as fixed a landmark as the clock tower or the old cherry tree that grows crookedly from the hillside. The tree was always being lopped; the clock often stopped. The peanut vendor seemed less perishable than the tree, more dependable than the clock. He had no family, but in a way all the world was his family, because he was in continuous contact with people. And yet he was a remote sort of being; always polite, even to children, but never familiar. There is a distinction to be made between aloneness and loneliness. The peanut vendor was seldom alone; but he must have been lonely.

Summer nights he rolled himself up in a thin blanket

and slept on the ground, beside the dying embers of his fire. During the winter, he waited until the last show was over, before retiring to the coolies' shed where there was some protection from the biting wind.

Did he enjoy being alive? I wonder now. He was not a joyful person; but then, neither was he miserable. I should think he was a genuine stoic, one of those who do not attach overmuch importance to themselves, who are emotionally uninvolved, content with their limitations, their dark corners. I wanted to get to know the old man better, to sound him out on the immense questions involved in roasting peanuts all his life; but it's too late now. Today his dark corner was deserted; the old man had vanished; the coolies had carried him down to the cremation ground.

'He died in his sleep,' said the tea shop owner. 'He was very old.'

Very old. Sufficient reason to die.

But that corner is very empty, very dark, and I know that whenever I pass it I will be haunted by visions of the old peanut vendor, troubled by the questions I failed to ask.

~

Spoke to the Christian writers' group at Deodars, on the subject of writing for a living.

Question: Which, in your opinion, is the best book on Christianity?

'I'd always thought it was the New Testament,' was all I could say.

MAY

So now I'm sixty-seven. Time to pare life down to the basics of doing:

a) what I have to do
b) what I want to do

Much prefer the latter.

Siddharth (after reading my biodata): 'Dada, you were born in 1934! And you are still here!' After a pause: 'You are very lucky.'

I guess I am, at that.

Recently, at an airport hotel, the reception clerk asked me: 'And when did you arrive in India, sir?'

'On 19 May 1934,' I replied. 'I was flown in by a stork.'

~

H.H. (Her Highness) phoned to tell me that she gets sneezing fits in the middle of the night.

Told her it was all this nuclear dust flying around. Suggested that she try ginger tea, and rum instead of whisky.

I get sneezing fits too, but mostly during the day. Ganesh tells me it's a healthy sign. Apparently his father kept sneezing into a good old age.

H.H. phoned to say the sneezing had stopped. 'Must have been the ginger tea,' I said. 'Rum and ginger,' she said. 'That did it.'

~

The rich and the famous have taken over Landour. The locals take them in their stride, and the tea shop owners and stray dogs are happy with this sudden advent of affluence, but my Bank Manager is dissatisfied. The rich folk won't keep their money here, he tells me. Can't blame them, I suppose. It's a place where everyone knows what you have in your account.

When I first came to live in Mussoorie, some forty years ago, I did not expect to be the only writer living in or around the hill station. There were, of course, writers in Dehradun, which had a literary climate of sorts; but in

Mussoorie there was none, at least not until I'd been here for some time.

Hugh Gantzer belongs to Mussoorie, but in the 1960s he was still serving with the Indian navy and I did not meet him till 1970 or thereabouts, at which time he was writing short stories. It was only after his retirement from the navy that he and his wife became a team of highly successful travel writers. And so, naturally they travelled: 'From Brazil to Zanzibar/They would feast on caviar!' as I once told them. And perhaps they'll bring me some too.

It was in the early 1970s that the first 'budding' writer came my way—a young man of American parentage but born and educated in Mussoorie. He told me that he planned to write a novel in due course, and I nodded sympathetically and made encouraging sounds. (The last time I had tried to discourage a would-be writer he became a critic and hounded me ever after!) A few years later this one did produce a novel. His name was Stephen Alter, and he went on to write a string of successful novels, which enabled him to kick the dust of Mussoorie from his heels and travel extensively. I believe he now lives in Cairo. Mussoorie's loss is Cairo's gain.

And who was the next friendly neighbourhood writer?

When I first met him he was wearing the orange robe of a sadhu, but he had a distinctive Scottish accent. He had spent twelve years in an ashram in Almora, and it definitely showed: he could eat nothing but porridge. He became secretary to the Rajmata of Jind. His name was Bill Aitken. One day he confessed to me that he was feeling bored and frustrated.

'Why don't you write something?' I suggested.

'Who'll publish it?'

'I will.' (I was then literary editor of *Imprint*, published from Bombay but compiled by me in Mussoorie.)

He wrote a story which duly appeared in the magazine, and after that there was no holding him back. Within a few years Bill was devouring railway tracks as though they were spaghetti, and writing more articles in a month than I could do in a year.

So I was not alone in the woods, after all.

Not with Win Chamberlain around. He was a gregarious American who looked a bit like Charles Bronson. He had written a sensational best-seller called *Gates of Fire*, set in an India difficult to recognize. Now he had rented a villa in Landour, where he was busy writing another, even more salacious novel. I forget the title, but this too must have been a best-seller, because he now has his own beach house in Goa. I shall have to write some raunchy stuff if I'm going to make much money.

Plodding on with my unsensational stories and children's books, I was made to feel even more of a country bumpkin when Dhiren Bhagat came along, flaunting a fat salary cheque from the *London Observer*, a retainer from the *London Spectator* and an advance from a London publisher. He was looking for a quiet place where he could write, he said. I helped him find a cottage, but he spent most of his time quarrelling with his landlady and did little serious writing there.

He was a charming young man in his early thirties, quite clever in his conversation. One of the first things he said to me was, 'Ruskin Bond—I thought you were dead!' I believe he had also written a premature obituary for Khushwant Singh.

Dhiren's feud with his landlady led him to leave his driver in charge of the cottage while he hared off to Delhi on a journalistic assignment. He was unaccustomed to Delhi's traffic, and on a busy road near Gole Market he met with a fatal accident. A great waste. In spite of his infuriating ways, he had real talent.

Since then, a number of interesting people have been flexing their muscles, dusting off their typewriters, and making me look and feel like a journeyman apprentice.

There's Victor Banerjee, who received an Academy Award nomination for his role in David Lean's *A Passage to India*. He writes enigmatic stories on his shiny new word processor. Ganesh Saili, on first-name terms with publishers, editors and TV celebrities, is always up to something new. He is a founder member of the Writers' Bar and the Landour Kennel Club. And of course there is a whole bunch of retired air marshals, brigadiers and surveyors with their formidable memoirs. I feel like a solitary wafer chip confronted by several club sandwiches.

We have got a publisher in our midst now the genial Pramod Kapoor of Roli Books whose fine house in Landour is often the scene of a jolly literary party, enlivened by the presence of a celebrity or two from New Delhi. The hillside rings with their laughter. And no one can complain of a lack of stimulus literary or otherwise.

~

My flower of the month: the poppy, while it lasts. A classic flower, extravagantly beautiful. The scarlet poppy is the most showy but I like the plain white as it makes for such a pleasing contrast. A pattern of poppies.

The unseasonal showers we have been having give today's poppies a rather bedraggled look, but there will be fresh blooms tomorrow.

There's an old saying: 'Pluck poppies, make thunder.'

~

I guess we age without really knowing that it's happening.

Got up this morning, sat on the edge of my bed, went into a reverie, and ten minutes later found I was still sitting on the edge of my bed! Gautam looked in, stared at me for a few seconds and said, disbelievingly, 'You were a goalkeeper?'

Transferred myself to the parapet wall on the road. Professor Unniyal rode up on his scooter, stopped and remarked: 'Mr Bond, I recognized you from behind!'

'Well, thank you kind sir,' I said. 'Better to be recognized from behind than never to be recognized at all.'

~

A tiny warbler (Tikkell's yellow warbler, perhaps) came in at the window and couldn't find its way out. Tired from beating its wings against the glass, it allowed itself to be taken by Siddharth in his hand. When we went outside, it remained seated on Sid's finger for some time, before suddenly realizing that it was free. It darted into the plum tree, and then into the oak forest, where presumably it rejoined its fellow warblers.

~

Attended a Bollywood-style celebration at my favourite hotel—the Savoy, naturally!

The songs and dances were a little too much for me, but I was sustained through the evening by generous libations of liquor provided by a very solicitous waiter.

After some time, I discovered that all the waiters were tipsy, although no one else seemed to notice this until dinner time when the dinner failed to put in an appearance. A power failure further complicated matters. There was one candle for a roomful of fifty people. Dinner was eventually served in the dark, and I heard one woman exclaim: 'This chicken is delicious!'

'That's the vegetable marrow, my dear,' said her companion. 'I don't think the chicken ever got here.'

When the lights came on, there was a fight between staff and guests, probably over the missing chicken curry. A storm outside added to the surreal atmosphere. Liquor bottles were mysteriously empty, waiters having helped themselves during the blackout. But more bottles and chickens appeared, and everyone agreed that it had been a great party and couldn't have been done better in Bombay.

A tip to those who want to throw a really 'fun' party: Make sure the waiters have plenty to drink.

~

Though their numbers have diminished over the years, there are still a few compulsive daily walkers around: the odd ones, the strange ones, who will walk all day, here, there and everywhere, not in order to get somewhere, but to escape from their homes, their lonely rooms, their mirrors, themselves ...

Those of us who must work for a living and would love to be able to walk a little more don't often get the chance. There are offices to attend, deadlines to be met, trains or planes to be caught, deals to be struck, people to deal with. It's the rat race for most people, whether they like it or not. So who are these lucky ones, a small minority it has to be said, who find time to walk all over this hill station from morn to night?

Some are fitness freaks, I suppose; but several are just unhappy souls who find some release, some meaning, in covering miles and miles of highway without so much as a nod in the direction of others on the road. They are not looking at anything as they walk, not even at a violet in a mossy stone.

Here comes Miss Romola. She's been at it for years. A retired schoolmistress who never married. No friends. Lonely as hell. Not even a visit from a former pupil. She could not have been very popular.

She has money in the bank. She owns her own flat. But she doesn't spend much time in it. I see her from my window, tramping up the road to Lal Tibba. She strides around the mountain like the character in the old song 'She'll be coming round the mountain', only she doesn't wear pink pyjamas; she dresses in slacks and a shirt. She doesn't stop to talk to anyone. It's quick march to the top of the mountain, and then down again, home again, jiggety-jig. When she has to go down to Dehradun (too long a walk even for her), she stops a car and cadges a lift. No taxis for her; not even the bus.

Miss Romola's chief pleasure in life comes from conserving her money. There are people like that. They view the rest of the world with suspicion. An overture of friendship will be construed as taking an undue interest in her assets. We are all part of an international conspiracy to relieve her of her material possessions! She has no servants, no friends; even her relatives are kept at a safe distance.

A similar sort of character but even more eccentric is Mr Sen, who used to live in the USA and walks from the Happy Valley to Landour (five miles) and back every day, in all seasons, year in and year out. Once or twice every week he will stop at the Community Hospital to have his blood pressure checked or undergo a blood or urine test. With all that walking he should have no health problems, but he is a hypochondriac and is convinced that he is dying of something or the other.

He came to see me once. Unlike Miss Romola, he seemed to want a friend, but his neurotic nature turned people away. He was convinced that he was surrounded by individual and collective hostility. People were always staring at him, he told me. I couldn't help wondering why, because he looked fairly nondescript. He wore conventional western clothes, perfectly acceptable in urban India, and looked respectable enough except for a constant nervous turning of the head, looking to the left, right, or behind, as though to check on anyone who might be following him. He was convinced that he was being followed at all times.

'By whom?' I asked.

'Agents of the government,' he said.

'But why should they follow you?'

'I look different,' he said. 'They see me as an outsider. They think I work for the CIA.'

'And do you?'

'No, no!' He shied nervously away from me. 'Why did you say that?'

'Only because you brought the subject up. I haven't noticed anyone following you.'

'They're very clever about it. Perhaps you're following me too.'

'I'm afraid I can't walk as fast or as far as you,' I said with a laugh; but he wasn't amused. He never smiled, never laughed. He did not feel safe in India, he confided. The saffron brigade was after him!

'But why?' I asked. 'They're not after me. And you're a Hindu with a Hindu name.'

'Ah yes, but I don't look like one!'

'Well, I don't look like a Taoist monk, but that's what I am,' I said, adding, in a more jocular manner: 'I know how to become invisible, and you wouldn't know I'm around. That's why no one follows me! I have this wonderful cloak, you see, and when I wear it I become invisible!'

'Can you lend it to me?' he asked eagerly.

'I'd love to,' I said, 'but it's at the cleaners right now. Maybe next week.'

'Crazy,' he muttered. 'Quite mad.' And he hurried on.

A few weeks later he returned to New York and safety. Then I heard he'd been mugged in Central Park. He's recovering, but doesn't do much walking now.

Neurotics do not walk for pleasure, they walk out of compulsion. They are not looking at the trees or the flowers or the mountains; they are not looking at other people (except in apprehension); they are usually walking away from something—unhappiness or disarray in their lives. They tire themselves out, physically and mentally, and that brings them some relief.

Like the journalist who came to see me last year. He'd escaped from Delhi, he told me. Had taken a room in Landour Bazaar and was going to spend a year on his own, away from family, friends, colleagues, the entire rat race. He was full of noble resolutions. He was planning to write an epic poem or a great Indian novel or a philosophical treatise. Every fortnight I meet someone who is planning to write one or the other of these things, and I do not like to discourage them, just in case they turn violent!

In effect he did nothing but walk up and down the mountain, growing shabbier by the day. Sometimes he recognized me. At other times there was a blank look on his face, as though he were on some drug, and he would walk past me without a sign of recognition. He discarded his slippers and began walking about barefoot, even on the stony paths. He did not change or wash his clothes. Then he disappeared; that is, I no longer saw him around.

I did not really notice his absence until I saw an ad in one of the national papers, asking for information about his whereabouts. His family was anxious to locate him. The ad carried a picture of the gentleman, taken in happier, healthier times; but it was definitely my acquaintance of that summer.

I was sitting in the Bank Manager's office, up in the cantonment, when a woman came in, making inquiries about her husband. It was the missing journalist's wife. Yes, said Mr Ohri, the friendly Bank Manager, he'd opened an account with them; not a very large sum, but there were a few hundred rupees lying to his credit. And no, they hadn't seen him in the bank for at least three months.

He couldn't be found. Several months passed, and it was presumed that he had moved on to some other town; or that he'd lost his mind or his memory. Then some milkmen from Kolti Gaon discovered bones and remnants of clothing at the bottom of a cliff. In the pocket of the ragged shirt was the journalist's press card.

How he'd fallen to his death remains a mystery. It's easy to miss your footing and take a fatal plunge on the steep slopes of this range. He may have been high on something or he may simply have been trying out an unfamiliar path. Walking can be dangerous in the hills if you don't know the way or if you take one chance too many.

And here's a tale to illustrate that old chestnut that truth is often stranger than fiction:

Colonel Parshottam had just retired and was determined to pass the evening of his life doing the things he enjoyed most: taking early morning and late evening walks, afternoon siestas, a drop of whisky before dinner, and a good book on his bedside table.

A few streets away, on the fourth floor of a block of flats, lived Mrs L, a stout, neglected woman of forty, who'd had enough of life and was determined to do away with herself.

Along came the Colonel on the road below, a song

on his lips, strolling along with a jaunty air; in love with life and wanting more of it.

Quite unaware of anyone else around, Mrs L chose that moment to throw herself out of her fourth-floor window. Seconds later she landed with a thud on the Colonel. If this was a Ruskin Bond story, it would have been love at first flight. But the grim reality was that he was crushed beneath her and did not recover from the impact. Mrs L, on the other hand, survived the fall and lived on into a miserable old age.

There is no moral to the story, any more than there is a moral to life. We cannot foresee when a bolt from the blue will put an end to the best-laid plans of mice and men.

JUNE

Typical Landour-Mussoorie morning:

No water in the taps.

No electricity until late afternoon.

Telephone out of order.

Postman comes by, but without any mail. Apparently the mail bus didn't turn up. Or rather, its driver went missing in Saharanpur.

The courier service boy didn't come either, because my neighbour's dog bit him last week.

Neighbour's dog is as vicious as its master. (Do we take after our dogs, or do they take after us?) Anyway, this one attacks people without provocation. I heard (on a BBC science programme) that chocolates are poison to dogs. So I fed the neighbour's dog an entire slab of

Cadbury's, but nothing happened; it kept coming around for more. So much for medical science. Must try Nestlé next time.

~

I may not love weeds (in the same sense that I love flowers), but I do respect and admire them basically, for their ability to flourish in the most unlikely and even hostile places, putting up with exhaust fumes, trampling feet, traffic, bulldozers, roadside tenements, grazing cattle and goats, giving one hope that not all the world's plant life will be extinct by the end of this century.

The dandelion growing on my retaining wall must be my flower of the month. It asserts its right to be there, where practically nothing else will flourish. Without any care or nourishment, it survives and grows strong and upright. Pluck it if you will, but there's no uprooting it from that space between two stones where it is so firmly embedded.

The dandelion opens its petals to the first rays of the sun and closes when the sunlight fades. And it is called Love's Oracle because of the custom of blowing on its puffball of seeds to discover whether 'She loves me' or 'She loves me not'. I have always been able to regulate my breath so as to obtain the answer I wanted!

~

I am frequently being asked to give some advice to budding writers. So here goes:

1. Make sure you can spell. If you can put a sentence together, that's even better.

2. Writing is not simply about words. Are you observant? Can you tell the difference between a sparrow and a sparrow-hawk?

3. Are you interested in anyone other than yourself? Writing about oneself has its limitations.

4. Are you prepared to wait years, maybe a lifetime, for recognition? If you want instant recognition, become a model.

5. If you're convinced that you are an unrecognized genius, remember this: everyone else feels the same way.

6. Writer's block. Everyone asks me about this. What do you do when stuck? That's easy. Just make sure the waste-paper basket is within throwing distance.

7. And finally, remember Red Smith's immortal words: 'Writing is very easy. All you have to do is sit in front of the typewriter till little drops of blood appear on your forehead.'

~

I did not feel like work this morning. And as it was raining there was nowhere to go. I tried reading a detective story, but it was one of those locked-room mysteries which usually try my patience. Gazing down at the road below didn't help because the rain had kept most people indoors. One of the simple pleasures of life is watering my plants, but Gautam had forestalled me; in fact, he'd drowned the geraniums. Another is browsing among old books, but I'd done that yesterday. So I sat down and made a list of 'simple pleasures', and came up with the following:

Listening to the cooing of doves and pigeons. But there are none in the vicinity. I remember an old well on the outskirts of Delhi; pigeons lived in the cool recesses of its walls. I wonder what happened to that well. The area is now a residential colony of multi-storeyed flats.

Watching blue jays (rollers) in flight, indulging in their aerial acrobatics. Another pleasure from the plains. I must get nearer home.

All right. Watching the sun come up from my bed near the window. But this morning there wasn't any sun!

Walking barefoot over dew-drenched grass. I'll keep it for another day.

Peeling an orange. Except that they're out of season.

Listening to street cries—sellers of balloons, candyfloss, pickles, gol-guppas—Gautam usually informs me of their approach. But today they are all waiting for the rain to stop.

Sometimes, on a walk, when I think no one is within hearing, I start singing some romantic ballad from the past. But I wish I'd taken voice training as a boy. This morning, in my room, I burst into song, and everyone came rushing to see what was wrong; they thought I was having some sort of fit.

This comes of listening to all those Nelson Eddy records when I was a boy. Only Gautam seems to appreciate my marching songs. He makes all the right noises, joining in and thumping on the table.

The rain stopped, the sun came out, and so did a swarm of yellow butterflies in compensation for the morning's absence of simple pleasures.

~

For nine months in the year only my closest friends come to see me. Then, when temperatures start soaring in the plains, long-lost friends suddenly remember me; and people whom I am barely able to recognize appear at the front door, willing to have me put them up for periods ranging from six days to six weeks. This is what comes of living in a hill station. I am a forgotten man until the holidays begin; then, suddenly, I am at the top of the popularity poll.

Sometimes I am master of the situation. I inform the hopeful visitors that the house is already bursting, that people are sleeping on the floor. If the hopefuls start looking around for signs of these uncomfortable residents, I remark that they have all gone out for a picnic.

The other day I received visitors who proved to be more thick skinned than most. The man was a friend of a friend of an acquaintance of mine. I'd never seen him before. But on the strength of this distant acquaintanceship, he'd brought his family along, together with their bedding rolls and other paraphernalia.

I tried the usual ploy; it did not work. The gentleman and his family were perfectly willing to share the floor space with any others who might be staying with me.

So I made my next move. 'I must warn you about the scorpions,' I said. 'Only yesterday I found a nest of scorpions beneath the carpet.'

The scorpion scare is effective with most people. But I was dealing with professionals. The man set his son to roll up the carpets, saying that they were the cause of the trouble. The lady switched on her transistor. Her husband made a call from his mobile.

'Sometimes centipedes fall from the ceiling,' I said desperately. 'And with the first shower of rain, there'll be giant leeches crawling in at the windows.'

They must have thought I was talking about the litchis that grow in Dehra, for they were unimpressed. The woman had begun to unpack. We were now interrupted by someone knocking on the front door. It was the postman, with two bulky sets of memoirs, and letters soliciting forewords or introductions to them. Their arrival inspired me to greater inventiveness.

'I'm very sorry,' I said, staring hard at one of these letters. 'I'm afraid I have to leave immediately for Rishikesh. A newspaper wants me to interview the Maharishi. I hope you won't mind. Would you like the name of a good hotel?'

'Are you taking your family too?' asked the woman.

'Er yes. Yes, of course!'

'It doesn't matter. We'll manage without them.'

'Oh, don't worry about us,' said the man expansively. 'We'll look after the house while you're away. It will be very hot in Rishikesh, but I suppose you have to go. You must return soon. Only do let us know when you're coming!'

~

Litchi time in the Doon. Sweet and sticky and irresistible. Ate almost as many as the children.

This is one of the few places in northern India where litchis can be grown. What's sad, though, is that the litchi orchards are fast disappearing. There's more money in selling the land to real estate agents, who do away with the litchi gardens and replace them with housing colonies and high-rise buildings. The guava trees disappeared long ago, and I suppose the mangoes will soon follow.

Nandu (of the Savoy) loves his mangoes. He can work his way through a couple of buckets in the course of a hot summer's day.

He also loves ice cream. I have been witness to his consumption of thirty-two cups of ice cream at a wedding feast. Next morning he was as green as his favourite pistachio ice cream.

Our mutual friend Ganesh chided him for his over-indulgence.

'They were only small cups,' said Nandu contritely.

I went to Barlowganj yesterday, a sleepy hollow a few kilometres from Landour. The only period when Barlowganj saw some excitement was when young 'Namkeen' (as his colleagues called him) arrived to take over as the manager of the little branch of a national bank.

Namkeen is one of those individuals with whom the more mischievous gods love to sport. A nervous gentleman, he seemed destined to have his nerves tested time and time again, even in Barlowganj.

On his first day in the bank, a masked man walked up to him, took out a revolver, and demanded that the contents of the safe be handed over. Namkeen obediently complied (as per banking procedure), handing over a couple of lakh rupees. The bandit then made a quick getaway. He was caught later, thanks to the presence of mind of a taxi driver; but the subsequent proceedings in court so tested the nerves of Namkeen that he declared he would rather deal with a bank robber than have the police constantly in and out of his home and office.

A month later, Namkeen's flat was burgled. More

policemen in and out of his flat. He applied for a transfer, which was turned down.

Then a reversing truck backed into his car. Namkeen got out just in time, but his car went over the edge and rolled down the hill until it was smashed to pieces on a rocky outcrop.

Namkeen had a nervous breakdown. A compassionate management finally gave him a transfer.

He is now quite happy in Dehradun, but refuses even to 'lift his eyes unto the hills', lest some fresh disaster descend on him. Barlowganj is peaceful again. Since he left, nothing of note has happened there. The new Bank Manager is a phlegmatic individual who offers no temptation to the subtle and malign influences that headed straight for Mr N. He bears out my theory that certain individuals are made for certain situations. Excitement will return to Barlowganj only when the innocent Namkeen comes that way again.

~

No night is so dark as it seems.

Here in Landour, on the first range of the Himalayas, I have grown accustomed to the night's brightness—moonlight, starlight, lamplight, firelight! Even fireflies and glow-worms light up the darkness.

Over the years, the night has become my friend. On the one hand, it gives me privacy; on the other, it provides me with limitless freedom.

Not many people relish the dark. There are some who will even sleep with their lights burning all night. They feel safer that way. Safer from the phantoms conjured up by their imaginations. A primeval instinct, perhaps, going back to the time when primitive man hunted by day and was in turn hunted by night.

And yet, I have always felt safer by night, provided I do not deliberately wander about on cliff tops or roads where danger is known to lurk. It's true that burglars and lawbreakers often work by night, their principal object being to get into other people's houses and make off with the silver or the family jewels. They are not into communing with the stars. Nor are late-night revellers, who are usually to be found in brightly lit places and are thus easily avoided. The odd drunk stumbling home is quite harmless and probably in need of guidance. I have often helped drunks find their way home, although I have yet to be thanked for it!

I feel safer by night, yes, but then I do have the advantage of living in the mountains, in a region where crime and random violence are comparatively rare. I know that if I were living in a big city in some other part of the world, I would think twice about walking home at midnight, no matter how pleasing the night sky.

Walking home at midnight in Landour can be quite eventful, but in a different sort of way. One is conscious all the time of the silent life in the surrounding trees and bushes. I have smelt a leopard without seeing it. I have seen jackals on the prowl. I have watched foxes dance in the moonlight. I have seen flying squirrels flit from one treetop to another. I have observed pine martens on their nocturnal journeys, and listened to the calls of nightjars and owls and other birds who live by night.

Not all on the same night, of course. That would be a case of too many riches all at once. Some night walks can be uneventful. But usually there is something to see or hear or sense. Like those foxes dancing in the moonlight. One night, when I got home, I sat down and wrote these lines:

> As I walked home last night,
> I saw a lone fox dancing
> In the bright moonlight.
> I stood and watched; then
> Took the low road, knowing
> The night was his by right.
> Sometimes, when words ring true,

I'm like a lone fox dancing
In the morning dew.

Who else, apart from foxes, flying squirrels, and night-loving writers, are at home in the dark?

Well, there are the nightjars, not much to look at, although their large, lustrous eyes gleam uncannily in the light of a lamp. But their sounds are distinctive. The breeding call of the Indian nightjar resembles the sound of a stone skimming over the surface of a frozen pond; it can be heard for a considerable distance. Another species utters a loud grating call which, when close at hand, sounds exactly like a whiplash cutting the air. 'Horsfield's nightjar' (with which I am more familiar in Mussoorie) makes a noise similar to that made by striking a plank with a hammer.

During the day the bird spends long hours sitting motionless on the ground, where it is practically invisible, only springing into life when an intruder approaches. It is also called the 'Goatsucker' because of its huge mouth and the legend spread in many countries that it feeds from the udders of cows and goats. Because of this erroneous belief, it is considered a bird of ill omen. Night-flying insects, such as moths and beetles, are its preferred meals.

I must not forget the owls, those most celebrated of night birds, much maligned by those who fear the night.

Most owls have very pleasant calls. The little jungle owlet has a note which is both mellow and musical. One misguided writer has likened its call to a motorcycle starting up, but this is a libel. If only motorcycles sounded like the jungle owl, the world would be a more peaceful place to live and sleep in.

Then there is the little scops owl, who speaks only in monosyllables, occasionally saying 'Wow' softly but with great deliberation. He will continue to say 'Wow' at intervals of about a minute, for several hours throughout the night.

Probably the most familiar of Indian owls is the spotted owlet, a noisy bird who pours forth a volley of chuckles and squeaks in the early evening and at intervals all night. Towards sunset, I watch the owlets emerge from their holes one after another. Before coming out, each puts out a queer little round head with staring eyes. After they have emerged they usually sit very quietly for a time as though only half awake. Then, all of a sudden, they begin to chuckle, finally breaking out in a torrent of chattering. Having in this way 'psyched' themselves into the right frame of mind, they spread their short, rounded wings and sail off for the night's hunting.

I wend my way homewards. 'Night with her train of stars' is always enticing. The poet Henley found her so. But he also wrote of 'her great gift of sleep', and it is this gift that I am now about to accept with gratitude and humility. For it is also good to be up and dancing in the morning dew.

~

There are two giant deodars in front of the Savoy, and they must be at least two hundred years old. That makes them older than the hill station. They have stood there as mute witnesses to the history of the town, and have watched the comings and goings of all kinds of people— soldiers, princes, memsahibs, rickshaw pullers, crorepatis, paupers, the lot.

A couple of old rickshaws are still parked near the hotel gate, and one night, for a lark, we seated Nandu in one of them, and Ganesh and I pulled and pushed and took him for a ride around the deserted tennis courts. Nandu enjoyed the ride so much that he now feigns a limp in order to persuade us to take him for further rides. If, on your late night walk, you should see a distinguished looking gentleman in a rickshaw pulled by two stout, well-nourished rickshaw wallahs, it is not Kipling's 'phantom rickshaw', it's the real thing!

~

The barbet is one of those birds which are heard more often than they are seen. Summer visitors to Shimla, Mussoorie and other north Indian hill resorts will be familiar with its monotonous, far-reaching call, 'pee-oh, pee-oh'. It keeps to the tops of high trees, where it is not easily distinguished from the foliage.

Like politicians, barbets love listening to their own voices, and often two or three birds answer each other from different trees, each trying to outdo the other in a shrill shouting match. Most birds are noisy during the mating season. Barbets are noisy all the year round.

There are some who like the barbet's call and consider it both striking and pleasant. Others don't like it and simply consider it striking.

Up here in Garhwal Himalayas there is a legend that the bird is the reincarnation of a money-lender who died of grief at the unjust termination of a lawsuit. Eternally his plaint rises to heaven, 'Un-ee-ow, un-ee-ow', which means 'Injustice, injustice!'

So the barbet's call can be interpreted in various ways. To me it always sounds like 'Pakrao, pakrao!'— 'Catch him, catch him!' And of course there has to be a story about how a barbet helped to catch a thief.

That the Doon is well forested today is due mainly to the early efforts of the Forest Department. Up to 1864 a free system of felling was prevalent, and we find Mr O'Callaghan, Deputy Conservator of Forests, writing in 1879:

> There can be no doubt that sal, tun and shisham were the trees chiefly felled, for even now there is no demand for any other kind of timber; and when I entered the department in 1854 the ground was everywhere studded with stumps of those trees.

Restrictions were gradually imposed, but no real conservation was attempted until the 1880s. By then, all that was valuable had already been cut, and the main duty of the department was to encourage replanting and foster new generations of trees those very trees which conservationists are striving to protect today.

Those who look with horror upon the denudation of our hills might well look back on the situation that confronted a settlement officer over a hundred years ago. In the Jaunsar area, all misfortunes were believed to be due to the machinations of one or other of their demon spirits; and in the *Gazetteer* of that period we read that the 'people of Chijal, being afflicted with smallpox, burnt down four hundred deodar trees as a sacrifice'.

Monsoon

JULY

Now that the rains are here, the occasional snake, flooded out of its home, makes its appearance on the road or hillside.

Most of the snakes up here are perfectly harmless, carrying only enough venom to paralyse their natural prey, which consists of frogs, rats, earthworms, small birds and smaller snakes.

Recently I saw two pretty green and brown snakes on the hillside. I have no idea what they are called; I cannot pretend to be an expert on recognizing all the denizens of the wild, and never cease to wonder at the sharp-eyed observations of well-known naturalists who can tell a bullfinch from a chaffinch at a distance of sixty metres, or distinguish a pit viper from a saw-scaled viper in one hurried glance. I suspect some of them are just showing off. The experts, I mean. Snakes do not show off.

However, as regards the snakes on my hillside, I can say with certainty that one is brown and one is green; and personally I prefer the green one.

The postman, who almost trod on it the other day, wanted it killed; but I quoted the sayings of Buddha, Krishna and Confucius, and persuaded him to let it live. In some former incarnation it might well have been related to us, I said. Perhaps an aunt or distant cousin. He wasn't quite convinced, and nor was I, but it gave the snake enough time in which to slip away. The postman no longer enters at the gate, but leaves my letters in a hole in the wall.

~

Our insect musicians are roused to their greatest activity during the monsoons. At dusk the air seems to tinkle and murmur to their music. To the shrilling of the grasshoppers is added the staccato notes of the crickets, while in the grass and on the trees myriads of lesser artistes are producing a variety of sounds.

As musicians, the cicadas are in a class of their own.

Throughout the monsoons their screaming chorus rings through the forest. A shower, far from dampening their ardour, only rouses them to a deafening crescendo of effort.

As with most insect musicians, the males do the performing, the females remain silent. This moved one chauvinistic Greek poet to exclaim: 'Happy the cicadas, for they have voiceless wives!' To which I would respond by saying, 'Pity the female cicadas, for they have singing husbands!'

Probably the most familiar and homely of insect singers are the crickets. I won't attempt to go into detail on how the cricket produces its music, except to say that its louder notes are produced by a rapid vibration of the wings, the right wing usually working over the left, the edge of one acting on the file of the other to produce a shrill, long-sustained note, like a violinist gone mad. Cicadas, on the other hand, use their abdominal muscles to produce their sound.

One of our best-known crickets is a large black fellow who lives underground and rarely comes out by day, except when the rain floods him out of his burrow.

But when night falls he sits on his doorstep and pours out his soul in strident song. This troubadour's name is as impressive as his sound—*Brachytrypes portentasus*.

The mole cricket is a genius by itself. It is a tiller of the soil. It uses its powerful fore limbs to shovel up the earth and its hard head for butting into it. Notwithstanding its earthly occupations, the mole cricket is sometimes moved to music. But as he repeats his note, a solemn deep-toned chirp (more burp than chirp) about a hundred times a minute, the performance can be monotonous.

And finally there are the tree crickets, a band of willing artistes who commence their performance at dusk. Their sounds are familiar, but it is difficult to see the musicians. A tap on the bush upon which one of them sits will bring an immediate end to the performance.

I wish the tree crickets would duet, in the manner of Nelson Eddy and Jeanette Macdonald. But it is only the males who sing, in order to please their consorts.

And speaking of Nelson Eddy, this is the hundredth anniversary of his birth. A fine baritone, unjustly neglected. When I listen to his songs (on tape or disk), the crickets and cicadas maintain a respectful silence. I'm sure they are listening.

I grew up on his songs. I still listen to them, especially my favourites, which are the songs based on poems:

Trees (Joyce Kilmer)
Invictus (William Ernest Henley)
Tomorrow (Amal Dunqul)
Boots (Rudyard Kipling)
Route Marching (Rudyard Kipling)
The Road to Mandalay (Rudyard Kipling)
Shadrack (Keith Preston)

~

The rains have heralded the arrival of some seasonal visitors: a leopard and several thousand leeches.

Heard that a leopard had carried off a dog at Sisters Bazaar. How can I induce it to come down here and seize my neighbour's dog? Old Colonel Powell (now gone to his maker) taught me how to make a passable leopard call, but it turned out to be a mating call and we attracted a pair of very excited young leopards. The Colonel and I beat a hasty retreat.

Which reminds me of the 'Introduction' I once wrote for a book called *The Maneater of Dogadda*, a factual account with photographs. The printers got the captions mixed up, and there appeared a picture of a dead leopard with the caption 'Well-known writer Ruskin Bond writes an introduction' and a picture of me with the caption 'Dreaded maneater after it was shot'. The latter was the more convincing.

How did Sisters Bazaar come by its name? Well, in the bad old, good old days, when Landour was a convalescent station for sick and weary British soldiers, the nursing sisters had their barracks in the long, low building that lines the road opposite Prakash's Store. On the old maps this building is called 'The Sisters'.

Of a bazaar there is little evidence, although Prakash's Store must be at least a hundred years old. It is famous for its homemade cheese, and tradition has it that several generations of the Nehru family have patronized the store, from Motilal Nehru in the 1920s, to others in more recent times.

I am more of a jam-fancier myself, and although I no longer live in the area, I do sometimes drop into the store for a can of raspberry or apricot or plum jam, made from the fruit brought here from the surrounding villages.

Further down the road is Dahlia Bank, where dahlias once covered the precipitous slope (known as the

'Eyebrow'). The old military hospital (which was opened in 1827) has been altered and expanded to house the present Defence Institute of Technological Management. Beyond it lies Mount Hermon, with the lonely grave of a lady who perished here one wild and windy winter, 150 years ago. And close by lies the lovely Oakville Estate, where at least three generations of the Alter family have lived.

~

The first time I truly experienced the joy of reading was one monsoon, many years ago. We had moved again. My stepfather was supporting my mother once more, so she had given up the managerial job at the small hotel that was about to close down anyway. They had rented a small, rather damp bungalow on Dehra's Canal Road, and I had a dark little room which leaked at several places when it rained.

'Lonely!' exclaimed Thoreau, 'why should I feel lonely? Is not our planet in the Milky Way?'

The trouble was, we never saw the Milky Way for the three months that the monsoons prevailed over Dehra. The rain thundered down, and when it wasn't raining, a fog descended on the town.

My room had a rather spooky atmosphere: the drip of water, the scurrying of rats in the space between the ceiling and corrugated tin roof, and the nightly visitation of a small bat who got in through a gap in the wall and swooped around the room, snapping up moths. I would stay up into the early hours, reading *Wuthering Heights* (all in one sitting, during a particularly stormy night—just the right atmosphere for it) or a work by Dickens, or Shakespeare's *Complete Works*. This lofty volume of Shakespeare's plays and poems was the only book in the house that I hadn't read till then. The print was very small, but I set myself the task of reading right through the entire tome, a feat which I achieved during the school holidays.

I realize now that my mother was a brave woman. She stuck it out with my stepfather, who, as a businessman, was a complete disaster. He'd lost his car agencies, his motor workshop, and was up against large income tax arrears. But this did not stop him and my mother from going off on hunting expeditions in the surrounding jungles, an expensive and time-consuming pastime.

Left largely to my own devices, I read whatever books came my way. Back in the 1940s, books were a scarce commodity in small-town India. There were hardly any libraries, and good bookshops were to be found only in the cities.

Poking around in the back veranda of my grandmother's house, at the other end of town, I found a cupboard full of books, untouched for years. I had never seen Granny read anything but religious tracts, which were always scattered about the house, so these must have been Grandfather's books. I borrowed them from time to time, and found much enjoyment in Pauline Smith's stories of South Africa, *The Little Karoo* and *The Big Karoo*, and *The Virginian* by Owen Wister, a novel that was a precursor of the modern 'Western'. There was also EHA's *Naturalist on the Prowl*, delightful sketches of Indian natural history; a great influence on me. It taught me to look twice at the natural world around me.

Back at my boarding school in Shimla (Bishop Cotton's), I found a sympathetic soul in Mr Jones, an ex-army Welshman who had been to school with my father and who taught us Divinity in class. He did not have the qualifications to teach us anything else, but I think I learnt more from him than from the teachers who had degrees after their names.

Mr Jones got on well with small boys, one reason being that he never punished them. Alone among the philistines, he was the one teacher to stand out against corporal punishment. He waged a lone campaign against the prevalent custom of caning boys for their misdemeanours, and in this respect was far ahead of his time. The other masters thought him a little eccentric, and he lost his seniority because of his refusal to administer physical punishment.

But there was nothing eccentric about Mr Jones, unless it was the pet pigeon that followed him everywhere and sometimes perched on his bald head. He had a passion for the works of Dickens, and when he discovered that I had read *Oliver Twist* and *Sketches by Boz*, he allowed me to borrow from his set of the *Complete Works* with the illustrations by Phiz. I launched into *David Copperfield*, which I thoroughly enjoyed, identifying myself with young David, his tribulations and triumphs. After reading *Copperfield*, I decided it would be a fine thing to become a writer. The seed had been sown, and although, in my imagination, I still saw myself as a football star or a Broadway tap dancer, I think I knew in my heart that I was best suited to the written word. I was topping the class in essay writing, and I was keeping a journal, something my father had taught me to do in the few happy years he'd been spared to me.

The school library was fairly well stocked, and I was put in charge of it. Here I worked my way through the plays of Barrie and Bernard Shaw, the novels and stories of Priestley, H.E. Bates, Maugham and Saroyan. After *Copperfield*, the novel that most influenced me was Hugh Walpole's *Fortitude*, an epic account of another young writer in the making. Its opening line still acts as a clarion call when I am depressed or feel as though I am getting nowhere. 'It isn't life that matters, but the courage you bring to it!' I returned to *Fortitude* last year and found it was still stirring stuff.

But school life wasn't all books. I excelled as a football goalkeeper, and since then guarding my goal, my way of life, has always been my forte. I was in the school choir, but was told not to sing, because I had a terrible singing voice. Apparently I looked quite cherubic in a cassock and surplice, and was told by our choirmistress to open my mouth along with the others, but on no account to allow any sound to issue forth! No wonder I became an admirer of Nelson Eddy, a singer in the classical mould.

Mr Jones helped me to overcome my fear of water and taught me to swim a little. He taught me the breaststroke, saying it was more suited to my quiet, reflective temperament. He hadn't seen my temper tantrums, which were usually reserved for home!

AUGUST

Thousands converge on the town from outlying villages, for a local festival. By late evening, scores of drunks are staggering about on the road. A few fights, but largely good-natured.

The women dress very attractively and colourfully, but for most of the menfolk the height of fashion appears to be a new pyjama-suit. But I'm a pyjama person myself. Pyjamas are comfortable. And I like them with stripes.

When I wear my old black dressing gown, Gautam calls me 'Batman'.

I stood tall and said, 'I was a goalkeeper once. I could dive all over the place.'

'Show me,' he said.

I made a dive across the carpet, and banged my knee on a wretched side table.

'That was a good dive,' said Gautam, 'but you hit the goalpost.'

~

To me, flowers are the most sensual of living things, or perhaps it's just that they appeal to the sensuality in my own nature. A rose in bud, the heady scent of jasmine, the unfolding of a lily, the flaunting colours of dahlias and giant marigolds, the seductive fragrance of the honeysuckle, all these excite and entice me.

A wild species of geranium (the round-leafed cransebill, to give its English name) with a tiny lilac flower, has responded to my overtures, making a great display in a tub where I encouraged it to spread. Never one to spurn a gesture of friendship, I have given it the freedom of the shady back veranda. Let it be my flower of the month, this rainy August.

~

Invited to a dinner at the Savoy to meet a group of senior bureaucrats from a neighbouring state. As transport had been provided for me, I arrived a bit early, and was standing near the reception when the other invitees arrived.

The first arrival, on being introduced, asked me if I was the owner of the hotel. As I am not as handsome as Nandu, I felt quite flattered.

The second arrival shook my hand vigorously, then proclaimed, 'Yes, of course, I've read your book *No Full Stops in India*!'

'That was Mark Tully,' I snapped. 'He smokes a pipe.'

The third or fourth arrival got it right, but spoilt it all by asking, 'Do you still write, Mr Bond?'

This is like asking a chef if he still makes soup, or a cobbler if he can repair a shoe. I couldn't be bothered answering his question, but a little boy came to my rescue by asking me to sign my latest book.

Nevertheless, the question lingers and sometimes I ask myself: Did I find my dream—the dream of forty-five years ago? Do I remember that dream?

Most of it, I do believe.

To live independently as a full-time writer; that was part of the dream. And I have done that for most of my adult life. No riches, no houses, no cars, no computers. But independence, certainly.

To live in the place of my choice. While I was toiling away in Delhi in the early 1960s, I decided I was going to live in the hills and work from there. Just as, five years earlier, I had decided that home was India and not England.

Mussoorie may not have been the perfect choice (there are places more lovely), but in many ways it has suited me. I'm near the Doon (familiar territory), not too far from Delhi (and my publishers, who tremble at my approach), and just a short walk into the solitude of the mountains.

I have lived with the family and companions of my choice—Prem and his children and grandchildren, and many good people on the hillside who have been generous to me over the years.

And have I won the time for leisure, books, nature, love and friendship? Yes, most of it, these things for some of the time. Not everything falls neatly into place. How can it? But I think I've done most of what I set out to do. I could have done it a little better and perhaps there's time to do more. My faults and limitations are many, but I've always accepted that I'm a most imperfect specimen of humanity, which means I've always been on friendly terms with myself!

And yes sir, I'm still doing my thing: cobbling shoes, making a tolerable soup, and recording my life and the life around me to the best of my ability.

~

Talking of hotels, most of them, big or small, have one thing in common: the occasional guest who makes off with the linen, the cutlery, and sometimes even a TV set.

Nandu (of the Savoy) tells of how one customer drove off with a mattress rolled up on the luggage rack. When the manager realized what had happened, he phoned the police at the toll barrier, and they stopped the car and took possession of the mattress. The owner of the car promptly blamed his driver for the theft, but the driver responded, 'Sir, you asked me to pick up two mattresses, and now you are blaming me for stealing one!'

Of course there are some tourists who leave their belongings behind; or if not their belongings, their fellow travellers. The day after a group of jolly, beer-guzzling young men vacated their room, the housekeeper opened a cupboard to have a dead body tumble out on top of her. In a different hotel, a box bed was found stuffed with a decaying corpse. Both cases went unsolved.

Equally enterprising were the young men from Haryana who stabbed to death one of their companions and left the body in the Landour cemetery. But these gentlemen left so many clues behind that they were caught a few days later.

Nandu is always leaving his keys behind in Bangalore. The last time he did this, we arranged for a lock picker to come up from Dehra and open Nandu's locked cupboards, trunks, desks etc. Nandu put new locks on all of them. Then, in a fit of anxiety, he stayed up all night, just in case the lock picker should return!

Hill stations are, by and large, peaceful places, but just occasionally crime rears its ugly head and an old lady is found strangled in her bed or a failed businessman is found hanging in the bathroom.

We won't dwell on these tragedies but think instead of the thousands who come here in high spirits and go away in even better spirits, the combination of clean mountain air, breathtaking scenery, and, just occasionally, spirits of the bottled variety having done wonders for their outlook on life.

~

Having just read a nasty review of my last book in *India Today*, I take heart by recalling Hemingway's direct action against critic Max Eastman in 1937. Eastman had questioned Hemingway's manhood in his review of *Death in the Afternoon*, which he had sarcastically titled 'Bull in the Afternoon'.

When Hemingway saw Eastman, he bashed him over the head with a copy of the book and then wrestled him to the ground. Trouble is, my critic is a woman. I'd lose the wrestling match.

This sort of response is rare, but exchanges between authors and critics can get nasty, with reputations maligned and genuine talents belittled. The worst sort of reviewers are those who make personal attacks on authors, usually a sign of envy coupled with malice. Thomas Carlyle called Emerson 'a hoary-headed and toothless baboon' and wrote of Charles Lamb: 'a more pitiful, rickety, gasping, staggering Tomfool I do not know.' But we still read and enjoy Lamb and Emerson; who reads Carlyle?

Of Walt Whitman, one reviewer said: 'Whitman is as unacquainted with art as a hog is with mathematics.' Swift was accused of having 'a diseased mind' and Henry James was called an 'idiot and a Boston idiot to boot, than which there is nothing lower in the world'. Their critics have long been forgotten, but just occasionally an author turns critic with equal virulence. There was the classic Dorothy Parker review which read: 'This is not a novel to be tossed aside lightly. It should be thrown with great force.'

When brickbats are flung at an author it is usually a sign that he or she is successful, has reached the top. No one received more abuse than Shakespeare. *Hamlet* was described by Voltaire as 'the work of a drunken savage', and Pepys said *A Midsummer Night's Dream* was 'the most insipid, ridiculous play that I ever saw in my life'. Macaulay sneered at Wordsworth's 'crazy mystical metaphysics, the endless wilderness of dull, flat, prosaic twaddle', a description that would aptly describe Macaulay's own meandering and monotonous style.

Should authors really have to put up with this sort of thing? Politicians do, and actors and sportsmen, so why not writers? As E.M. Forster once said: 'No author has the right to whine. He was not obliged to be an author. He invited publicity, and he must take the publicity that comes along.'

Of course, some reviewers do go a little too far, like the one who once referred to 'that well-known typist Harold Robbins'.

That was a remark truly deserving a bash over the head, on behalf of typists everywhere.

~

Blood pressure up and down.

Writing for a living: it's a battlefield!

People do ask funny questions. Accosted on the road by a stranger, who proceeds to cross-examine me, starting with: 'Excuse me are you a good writer?' For once, I'm stumped for an answer.

~

It is the last day of August, and the lush monsoon growth has reached its peak. The seeds of the cobra lily are turning red, signifying that the rains are coming to an end.

In a few days the ferns will start turning yellow, but right now they are still firm, green and upright. Ground orchids, mauve lady's slipper and the white butterfly orchids put on a fashion display on the grassy slopes of Landour. Wild dahlias, red, yellow and magenta, rear their heads from the rocky crevices where they have taken hold.

Snakes and rodents, flooded out of their holes and burrows, take shelter in roofs, attics and godowns. A shrew, weak of eyesight, blunders about the rooms, much to the amusement of the children.

'Don't kill it,' admonishes their grandmother. '*Chuchundars* are lucky—they bring money!'

And sure enough, I receive a cheque in the mail. Not a very large one, but welcome all the same.

The sun comes out for a few minutes, and then the mist climbs up from the valley and obscures the town and the hillside. I don't mind the mist. It does provide one with a certain amount of privacy. And for a brief while it conceals the garbage heaps that have become a feature of towns, large and small, all over northern India. As the human race multiplies, it becomes increasingly difficult to do away with its refuse. Not that anyone really tries.

At the bottom of the hill, far from the madding crowds, there is a small rippling stream, its water almost hidden by the bright green tangled growth along its course. It is only by its sound as it chatters over the pebbles that we become aware of it. Here we find many small plants that delight in growing in such places: water mint, wild strawberries, wood sorrel, violets and dandelions, and a forest of ferns.

Many popular flower names suggest that people were more interested in a plant's taste than its appearance. Wood sorrel and sorrel dock share a name that means sour. Wood sorrel was once used in salads, and sorrel dock was eaten with mutton. There is no reason why they should not still be used this way, except that people have lost the habit of walking about in search of herbs. In England, the broad-leaved pepperwort was used before pepper became common; and it's a nicer name than *Lepidum Smithii* (Smith's scaly plant). John Ruskin, in a bad mood, said that some plants were named after diseases, some after vermin, some after blockheads (meaning botanists) and the rest anyhow.

And here's an old proverb which I had put down in one of my notebooks, long ago:

'He who seeks the herb for its cure, will find it half effected by the walk.'

In earlier times plants were called simples, by which was meant a simple medicine, as opposed to a compound. As each illness had a herb to cure it, simples were preferred to compounds. The word drug is said to mean dried plant, and many medicinal plants were sold in shops; some people preferred to gather their own samples, deriving extra benefit from the exercise involved.

According to the Doctrine of Signatures, plants

themselves gave some indication of their usefulness. A walnut, having a hard shell like a skull and a kernel configured like a brain, signified that it was a cure for all troubles of the head! And if apples were good for the heart, grapes were a sure cure for piles. But what was there about maidenhair fern to suggest a cure for baldness? One would have thought skullcap better, but that was a cure for insomnia.

To return to the stream at the bottom of the hill, the maidenhair is certainly one of the loveliest ferns to be found near running water. It grows from rocks, in sheltered places, protected from sun and wind. If plunged in water, it always remains dry. The early botanists, who loved to classify plants by Latinizing their names, were quite happy to adopt the honest English folk name of 'maiden hair', meaning pubic hair. The prudish Victorians tried changing the name, but to no avail.

Another beautiful group of ferns growing almost to the water are the lady ferns, whose broad fronds are often four to five feet high. They are almost transparent in the fineness of their foliage, looking so tender that you would think the sun and wind would scorch or shrivel them up. But the constant presence of flowing water keeps them cool and fresh.

When the frosts of winter come, the fronds will

crumple up into a heap of brown fragments. But their strength has by that time returned into the thick clump of roots, to be stored and used for a still finer group of fronds next year.

In the moist parts of any forest there are sure to be several other kinds of ferns such as the male fern, whose strong, upright fronds make it look like a large green shuttlecock three feet high.

There are several hundred varieties of ferns, and their history goes back to the mists of antiquity. There was a time when ferns and plants like them filled the earth. It was a wet and dripping time. Flowers would have been of no use at all, but spores could carry on their lives in the prevailing dampness. Some ferns grew as large as trees.

The ferns are not the only interesting plants near our stream. Rambling over the hillside are the wild dog roses which send out very long branches, covered with broad, strong hooks by which they climb over the hedges in all directions. Throughout the spring and early summer the climber is covered with lovely, sweet-smelling pink or white flowers which in the autumn change to scarlet berries known as 'hips'.

'Why is it called the dog rose?' asked Siddharth. 'It doesn't bark and it doesn't wag its tail.'

I had to confess to being equally mystified. What had this pretty wild rose in common with a dog? I found the answer in an old herbal: it is the translation of a Greek name that means a cure for hydrophobia. Apparently a decoction of the root was administered to someone bitten by a dog.

In early flower lore, the names of flowers also had secret or mystical meanings: thyme for truth, rosemary for remembrance, roses for love, heartsease for joy, and so on. No flower was without a sentimental meaning, and it was possible to send letters of passion, friendship or reproach, 'without inking the fingers'. Lady Mary Montague, during her travels, sent her absent lover a love letter which carried these interpretations with her gift of Eastern flowers and spices:

Clove: I have long loved you and you have not known it.

Jonquil: Have pity on my passion.

Pear blossom: Give me some hope.

Rose: May you be pleased, and your sorrows be mine.

Straw: Suffer me to be your slave.

Cinnamon: My fortune is yours.

Pepper: Send me an answer.

Shakespeare knew the language of flowers, and he put their interpretation into the poor mad head of Ophelia:

> There's rosemary, that's for remembrance—pray you, love, remember. And there is pansies, that's for thoughts ... There's fennel for you; and columbines. There's rue for you. And here's some for me ... You must wear your rue with a difference. There's a daisy. I would give you some violets, but they withered all when my father died ...

Autumn

SEPTEMBER

Month began with a cheque that bounced.

Refrained from checking my blood pressure, although I snapped at everyone except Gautam. It's impossible to snap at Gautam. Drank ginger tea for my headache; then one of Ganesh's cocktails.

~

It was someone in *Three Men in a Boat* who, having read through a medical encyclopaedia, came to the conclusion that he suffered from every ailment described in the book with the possible exception of housemaid's knee. Having been something of a hypochondriac myself when I was younger, I can sympathize with him.

What is housemaid's knee, anyway? Never having examined one myself, I looked it up, and discovered that it is a swelling of the bursa (nothing to do with a bursar) in front of the kneecap, due, as the name suggests, to excessive pressure from kneeling. As housemaids no longer kneel, and even kneeling in prayer is out of fashion, the disease would appear to have died out. Housemaids appear to have died out too.

One of the better-known ailments from which hypochondriacs often suffer is constipation. Two constipated days, and they feel that the world (theirs, anyway) is coming to an end. They then proceed to poison themselves with all the purgatives they can lay hands on. If it's any consolation to sufferers from habitual constipation, I quote the following from the *Pears Medical Encyclopaedia*: 'There are quite a number of people who have movements about five or six times a year, yet their general health remains good.' I find this hard to believe, but there it is, on the authority of the medical profession.

My grandmother was a great believer in fresh fruit juices as a cure for many ailments, and it is true that in the case of constipation a diet of papayas and grape juice was an effective and popular cure with her grandchildren.

Not all Grandmother's cures were equally effective. When Grandfather was losing hair rather rapidly, she came up with a cure for baldness. This consisted of onions pickled in gin, the resultant lotion to be massaged into the scalp morning and evening. Grandfather thought it did wonders: he threw the onions away and drank the gin.

Uncle Ken used this lotion on his scalp. He was chased around the house by a swarm of bees.

Massage itself is a good remedy for many ills of the body, and a good masseur is worth his worth in gold. I cannot help feeling a sneaking admiration for the masseur who would massage his clients to sleep with the rhythmic movements of his fingers before robbing them of their belongings. Such a person was arrested in Uttar Pradesh a year ago, and is presumably practising his skills on the weary limbs of his fellow convicts.

While I have never met this rhythmic masseur, I did know a man, an Australian of Italian extraction, who claimed to be a specialist in acupressure. Acupressure is like acupuncture, only you poke the patient with your fingers instead of with needles. He kept his nails long for this purpose.

When I told him I had a headache, he took me by the wrist and pressed down so hard on the tendons between my thumb and index finger that I yelped with pain. It's true the headache went away, but for a week my hand was swollen and bruised.

He suggested that in future I use my own fingertips in treating myself, and very kindly showed me all the pressure points on the body which I might explore with my fingertips in order to relieve pain in other parts of the body. Here's a sample cure: For travel sickness, you press down on a point just above the left ankle. The great thing about this cure is that, by the time you have located the exact point, the journey is over. So, in a way, it works.

In some countries there is a boom in health books, most of them aimed at hypochondriacs. There are those who live entirely on sprouted seeds, and for them there is *The Complete Sprouting Book*. For those who are afraid to eat anything at all there is *The Secret of Successful Fasting*. I am not making up these titles, they really do exist as do *Herbs to Soothe Your Nerves*, *The Healing Power of Pollen*, and Linda Clark's *Rejuvenation Programme for Reversing the Ageing Process*.

You can grow old just reading the titles.

~

Two dreams.

A constantly recurring one: I am forced to stay longer than I had intended in a very expensive hotel in a strange city and know that my funds are insufficient to meet the bill. Fortunately I have always woken up before the bill is presented!

Possible interpretation: Fear of insecurity. My own variation of the dream, common to many, of falling from a height but waking up before hitting the ground.

Another occasional dream: Living in a house perched over a crumbling hillside. This one is not far removed from reality! Our hillside is definitely slipping; the road below has a large crack down the middle.

~

Monsoon growth at its peak. The ladies' slipper orchids are falling off, but I noticed all the following wild flowers: balsam (two kinds), commelina, agrimony, wild geranium (very pretty), sprays of white flowers emanating from the wild ginger, the scarlet fruit of the cobra lily just forming, tiny mushrooms set like pearls in a retaining wall; ferns still green, which means more rain to come;

escaped dahlias everywhere; wild begonias and much else. The best time of the year for wild flowers.

Whose ghost was it that Ram Singh (the Savoy bartender) saw last night? A figure in a long black cloak, who stood for a few moments in the hotel's dimly lit vestibule, and then moved into the shadows of the old lounge. Ram Singh followed the figure, but there was no one in the lounge and no door or window through which the man (if it was a man) had made his exit.

Ram Singh doesn't tipple; or so he says. Nor is he the imaginative type.

'Have you seen this person—this ghost—before?' I asked him.

'Yes, once. Last winter, when I was passing the ballroom, I heard someone playing the piano. The ballroom door was locked, and I couldn't get in nor could anyone else. I stood on a ledge and looked through one of the windows, and there was this person—a hooded figure, I could not see the face—sitting on the piano stool. I could hear the music playing, and I tapped on the window. The figure turned towards me, but the hood was empty, there was nothing there to see! I ran to my room and bolted the door. We should sell that piano, sir. There's no one here to play it apart from the ghost.'

The clock over the Savoy bar is stationary at 8.20 and has been like that since the atomic bomb was dropped on Hiroshima over fifty years ago. That's what Nandu tells me, and I have no reason to disbelieve him. Many of his more outlandish statements often turn out to be true.

Almost any story about this old hotel in Mussoorie has a touch of the improbable about it, even when supported by facts. A previous owner, Mr McClintock, had a false nose—according to Nandu, who never saw it. So I checked with old Negi, who first came to work in the hotel as a room boy back in 1932 (a couple of years before I was born) and who, almost seventy years and two wives later, looks after the front office. Negi tells me it's quite true.

'I used to take McClintock sahib his cup of cocoa last thing at night. After leaving his room I'd dash around to one of the windows and watch him until he went to bed. The last thing he did, before putting the light out, was to remove his false nose and place it on the bedside table. He never slept with it on. I suppose it bothered him whenever he turned over or slept on his face. First thing in the morning, before having his cup of tea, he'd put it on again. A great man, McClintock sahib.'

'But how did he lose his nose in the first place?' I asked.

'Wife bit it off,' said Nandu.

'No, sir,' said Negi, whose reputation for telling the truth is proverbial. 'It was shot away by a German bullet during World War I. He got the Victoria Cross as compensation.'

'And when he died, was he wearing his nose?' I asked.

'No, sir,' said old Negi, continuing his tale with some relish. 'One morning when I took the sahib his cup of tea, I found him stone dead, without his nose! It was lying on the bedside table. I suppose I should have left it there, but McClintock sahib was a good man, I could not bear to have the whole world knowing about his false nose. So I stuck it back on his face and then went and informed the manager. A natural death, just a sudden heart attack. But I made sure that he went into his coffin with his nose attached!'

We all agreed that Negi was a good man to have around, especially in a crisis.

McClintock's ghost is supposed to haunt the corridors of the hotel, but I have yet to encounter it. Will the ghost be wearing its nose? Old Negi thinks not (the false nose being man-made), but then he hasn't seen the ghost at close quarters, only receding into the distance between the two giant deodars on the edge of the beer garden.

A lot of people who enter the Writers' Bar look pretty far gone, and sometimes I have difficulty distinguishing the living from the dead. But the real ghosts are those who manage to slip away without paying for their drinks.

I don't have to slip away. In the eight or nine years during which I have helped to prop up the Writers' Bar, I have seldom paid for a drink. That's the kind of friend I have in Nandu. You won't find a harsh word about him in these pages. I think he decided long ago that I was an adornment to the bar, and that, draped over a bar stool, I looked like Ray Milland in *The Lost Weekend*. (He won an Oscar for that.)

As for the Man from Sail, who is usually parked on the next bar stool, he's no adornment, in spite of the Jackie Shroff moustache. But I have to admit that he's skilful at pouring drinks, mixing cocktails and showing tipsy ladies to the powder room. He doesn't pay for his drinks either.

How, then, does dear Nandu survive? Obviously there are some real customers in the wings, and we help them feel at home, chatting them up and encouraging them to try the Royal Salute or even a glass of Beaujolais. I can rattle off the history of the hotel for anyone who wants to hear it; and as for the Man from Sail, he provides a free ambulance service for those who can't handle the hotel's hospitality. The Man from Sail is the town's number one blood donor, so if you come away from your transfusion with a bad hangover, you'll know whose blood is coursing around in your veins. But it's real Scotch, not the stuff they make at the bottom of the Sail mountain.

Nandu tells me that Pearl Buck, the Nobel laureate, stayed here for a few days in the early 1950s. I looked up the hotel register and found that he was right as usual. As far as I know, Miss Buck did not record her impressions of the hotel or the town in any of her books, though it's the sort of place people usually have something to say about. Like the correspondent of the *Melbourne Age* who complained because the roof had blown off his room during one of our equinoctial storms. A frivolous sort of complaint, to say the least. Nandu placated him by saying, 'Sir, in Delhi you can only get a five-star room. From your room here you can see all the stars!' And so he could, once the clouds had rolled away.

It's a windy sort of mountain, and in cyclonic storms our corrugated iron roofs are frequently blown away.

Old Negi recalls that a portion of the Savoy roof once landed on the St George's School flat, five miles away, at the height of a midsummer storm. In its flight it decapitated an early-morning fitness freak. Had anyone else told me the story, I wouldn't have believed it. But Negi's word is the real thing, as good as a sip of Johnnie Walker Blue Label.

OCTOBER

A good year for the cosmos flower. Banks of them everywhere. They like the day-long sun. Clean and fresh this month's flower, en masse. But by itself, the wild commelina, sky blue against dark green, always catches at the heart.

~

As a short-story writer, I have often found that railway stations and platforms give me some of my best stories. As there are now over 7,000 railway stations, in effect 7,000 destinations in India, I cannot complain of shortage of material. I have only to visit a railway station in order to experience first-hand that seething tide of life that is uniquely Indian. Mark Twain called it the 'perennially ravishing show of Indian railway stations'.

'Romance brought up the nine-fifteen,' wrote Rudyard Kipling, who was among the first to see the tremendous tourist potential of the Indian railways, and whose early (and best) stories were published in Wheeler's Indian Railway Library.

Anyone who has read his novel *Kim* (1901) will not forget the description of the long train journey undertaken by Kim and the Lama which took them from Lahore to Benaras:

> As the 3.25 a.m. south-bound roared in, the sleepers sprang to life, and the station filled with clamour and shouting, cries of water and sweetmeat vendors, shouts of policemen, and shrill yells of women gathering up their baskets, their families, and their husbands.

It's just over a hundred years since *Kim* was first published and it remains a best-seller to this day. More than in any of his works, *Kim* reveals Kipling's love and understanding of India.

The scene on a busy railway platform is much the same today, only more intensified: the travelling population has increased a hundredfold, and so has the number of trains. There are now over 7,500 trains operating in a single day, far exceeding the daily volume of traffic in any other country of the world.

In just one day these trains cover over 62,000 kilometres, a far cry from that historic occasion on 16 April 1853, when India's first train steamed off in an atmosphere of great excitement from Bori Bunder in Bombay to Thane, just thirty-four miles away. Crowds cheered, twenty-one guns boomed a salute, and the band played rousing tunes as the train's fourteen carriages carrying 400 special guests chugged slowly into the distance.

Fifty years later, soon after *Kim* was written, India was already criss-crossed by an extensive network of railway lines, bringing north to south and east to west, enabling a majority of Indians to discover the length, breadth and diversity of their country for the first time. Then, as now, we love to travel, especially by train, and every station, large or small, will provide a wonderful cross section of people: south Indians on their way to the great pilgrim centres of the north; north Indians travelling to the beautiful temples of the south; wedding parties thronging the platforms; soldiers going home on leave or returning to their regiments; gurus surrounded by throngs of disciples and followers; VIPs smothered in garlands.

I must confess to a personal weakness for railway platforms. Sometimes I buy a platform ticket just so that I can spend hours on a bench watching trains come and go, passengers arriving and departing, vendors plying their trade, luggage and goods of every description being moved mysteriously to different destinations. Guards blow their whistles, porters argue with passengers, and stationmasters lose their tempers. I am in empathy with stations and stationmasters. My maternal grandfather was a stationmaster on the old BB&CI Railway (Bombay, Baroda and Central Indian Railway), and perhaps that has something to do with it. There is still some engine soot in my blood.

There is nothing like an Indian railway station anywhere else in the world. We are not a melting pot of races and religions, we are a mosaic of all these things. A mosaic that is best observed from the trains that pull the glittering pieces together.

The Kangra Valley Railway is one of my own favourite journeys. This particular railway is visible proof that the railway construction engineer can create a work which is in complete harmony with the beauty of the surroundings. Without in any way interfering with the grandeur of mountain and valley, the railway engineers on this line have revealed to the traveller a land of great enchantment. The graceful curves of the rails, the neatness of the culverts, the symmetrical design of the bridges, the directness of the cuttings—all these help to throw into bold relief the ruggedness of the huge crags through which the line plays hide-and-seek.

By contrast, if you take the train to Shimla, you will spend half your time burrowing through the bowels of the earth with the scenic grandeur of the Himalayas blotted out from your vision and the hillsides made to resemble rabbit warrens.

Instead of boring his way through the mountains, the railway engineer in Kangra skilfully avoided running headlong into the hillside. Instead of following dizzy curves, he cleverly chose to avoid the awkward corners. He must have been a Taoist at heart, taking Nature's way rather than opposing it.

Not that I am averse to travelling by other mountain railways. Throughout my schooldays in Shimla, I was propelled up and down the mountain through those 103 soot-filled tunnels. When I grew up and had the choice, I took the railcar, which was cleaner, swifter and more comfortable. On the way up, it stopped at Barog, where an excellent breakfast was served. I believe the Barog breakfasts are as good as ever. And in December, on the way down, we would buy bunches of mistletoe at the station, for Barog was famous for its mistletoe. Those wayside stations always charmed me—Barog, Dharampur, Kandaghat, Tara Devi . . .

~

I am trying to recall that morning, forty-five years ago, when I saw my first novel in print. I was nineteen that year, and I had recently returned from England, where I had spent three years of drudgery in an office. I had done my writing in the evenings and at weekends, bombarding editors and publishers with my literary efforts. Eventually I had found a publisher. But on that sultry summer morning in Dehradun it wasn't the book I was looking out for (that came later), it was something else.

I was up a little earlier than usual, well before sunrise, well before my buxom landlady, Bibiji, called up to me to come down for my tea and paratha. It was going to be a special day and I wanted to tell the world about it. But when you're nineteen the world isn't really listening to you.

I bathed at the tap, put on a clean (but unpressed) shirt, trousers that needed cleaning, shoes that needed polishing. I never cared much about appearances. But I did have a nice leather belt with studs! I tightened it to the last rung. I was a slim boy, just a little undernourished.

On the streets, the milkmen on their bicycles were making their rounds, reminding me of William Saroyan, who sold newspapers as a boy, and recounted his experiences in *The Bicycle Rider in Beverley Hills*. Stray dogs and cows were nosing at dustbins. A truck loaded with bananas was slowly making its way towards the *mandi*. In the distance there was the whistle of an approaching train.

One or two small tea shops had just opened, and I stopped at one of them for a cup of tea. As it was a special day, I decided to treat myself to an omelette. The shopkeeper placed a record on his new electric record player, and the strains of a popular film tune served to wake up all the neighbours—a song about a girl's red dupatta being blown away by a gust of wind and then retrieved by a handsome but unemployed youth. I finished my omelette and set off down the road to the bazaar.

It was a little too early for most of the shops to be open, but the news agency would be the first and that was where I was heading.

And there it was: the National News Agency, with piles of fresh newspapers piled up at the entrance. The *Leader* of Allahabad, the *Pioneer* of Lucknow, the *Tribune* of Ambala, and the bigger national dailies. But where was the latest *Illustrated Weekly of India*? Was it late this week? I did not always get up at six in the morning to pick up the *Weekly*, but this week's issue was a special one. It was my issue, my special bow to the readers of India and the whole wide beautiful wonderful world. My novel was to be published in England, but first it would be serialized in India!

Mr Gupta popped his head out of the half-open shop door and smiled at me.

'What brings you here so early this morning?'

'Has the *Weekly* arrived?'

'Come in. It's here. I can't leave it on the pavement.'

I produced a rupee. 'Give me two copies.'

'Something special in it? Did you win first prize in the crossword competition?'

My hands were not exactly trembling as I opened the magazine, but my heart was in my mouth as I flipped through the pages of that revered journal—the one and only family magazine of the 1950s, the gateway to literary success—edited by a quirky Irishman, Shaun Mandy.

And there it was: the first instalment of *The Room on the Roof*, that naïve, youthful novel on which I had toiled for a couple of years. It had lively, evocative illustrations by Mario, who wasn't much older than me. And a picture of the young author, looking gauche and gaunt and far from intellectual.

I waved the magazine in front of Mr Gupta. 'My novel!' I told him. 'In this and the next five issues!'

He wasn't too impressed. 'Well, I hope circulation won't drop,' he said. 'And you should have sent them a better photograph.'

Expansively, I bought a third copy.

'Circulation is going up!' said Mr Gupta with a smile.

The bazaar was slowly coming to life. Spring was in the air, and there was a spring in my step as I sauntered down the road. I wanted to tell the world about my triumph, but was the world interested? I had no mentors in our sleepy little town. There was no one to whom I could go and confide: 'Look what I've done. And it was all due to your encouragement, thanks!' Because there hadn't been anyone to encourage or help, not then nor in the receding past. The members of the local cricket team, to which I belonged, would certainly be interested, and one or two would exclaim: '*Shabash*! Now you can get us some new pads and a set of balls!' And there were other friends who would demand a party at the *chaat* shop, which was fine, but would any of them read my book? Readers were not exactly thick on the ground, even in those pre-television, pre-computer days. But perhaps one or two would read it, out of loyalty.

A cow stood in the middle of the road, blocking my way.

'See here, friend cow,' I said, displaying the magazine to the ruminating animal. 'Here's the first instalment of my novel. What do you think of it?'

The cow looked at the magazine with definite interest. Those crisp new pages looked good to eat. She craned forward as if to accept my offer of breakfast, but I snatched the magazine away.

'I'll lend it to you another day,' I said, and moved on.

I got on quite well with cows, especially stray ones. There was one that blocked the steps up to my room, sheltering there at night or when it rained. The cow had become used to me scrambling over her to get to the steps; my comings and goings did not bother her. But she was resentful of people who tried to prod or push her out of the way. To the delight of the other tenants, she had taken a dislike to the *munshi*, the property owner's rent collector, and often chased him away.

I really don't recall how the rest of that day passed, except that late evening, when the celebrations with friends were over, I found myself alone in my little room, trimming my kerosene lamp. It was too early to sleep, and I'd done enough walking that day. So I pulled out my writing pad and began a new story. I knew even then that the first wasn't going to be enough. Sheherazade had to keep telling stories in order to put off her execution. I would have to keep writing them in order to keep that munshi at bay and put off my eviction.

~

Composed a little jingle:

> I'm all right,
> I'm doing my thing,
> And in my own right
> I'm a king!

A walk in the twilight. Soothing. Watched the winter line from the top of the hill.

Winter

NOVEMBER

There is something in the air of the place—especially in October and November—that is conducive to romance and passion.

I read an entry in my journal written one November over a decade back:

> Fifty is a dangerous age for most men. There has been nothing to celebrate this year: only an abortive and unhappy love affair (dear reader, don't fall in love at fifty!). Skip being fifty. Become fifty-one as soon as possible; you will find yourself in calmer waters. If you fall in love at the age of fifty, inner turmoil and disappointment are almost guaranteed. Don't

listen to what the wise men say about love. P.G. Wodehouse said the whole thing succinctly: 'You know, the way love can change a fellow is really frightful to contemplate.' Especially when a fifty-year-old starts behaving like a sixteen-year-old!

~

Winter turns my mind to journeys those taken and those never done. Especially to a fantasy one I have always wanted to make: along the Grand Trunk Road from Calcutta to Peshawar.

For the Road is a river. It may not be as sacred as the Ganga, which it greets at Kanpur and Varanasi, but it is just as permanent. It's a river of life, an unending stream of humanity going places, intent on arriving and getting there most of the time.

A long day's journey into night that's how I would describe the saga of the truck driver, that knight errant, or rather errant knight, of India's Via Appia. Undervalued, underpaid and often disparaged, he drives all day and sometimes all night, carrying the country's goods and produce for hundreds of miles, across state borders, through lawless tracts, at all seasons and in all weathers. We blame him for hogging the middle of the road, but he is usually overloaded and if he veers too much to the left or right he is quite likely to topple over, burying himself and crew under bricks or gas cylinders, sugarcane or TV sets. More than the railwayman, the truck driver is modern India's lifeline, and yet his life is held cheap. He drinks, he swears, occasionally he picks up HIV, and frequently he is killed or badly injured. And we hate him for hogging the road. But we cannot do without him.

In the old, old days, when Muhammad Tughlaq, Sultan of Delhi, streamlined the country's roads, bullock carts and camel caravans were the chief transporters. In 1333, when the Moroccan traveller Ibn Battuta visited India, he was deeply impressed by the Sultan's road network. Sher Shah Suri, who ruled from 1540 till 1545, made further improvements, especially to the GT Road. He built caravansarais and inns for travellers, and planted fine trees along the GT Road and other important highways. Horsemen, carts and palanquin bearers jostled for pride of position, much as our motorists do today. Traffic was slow moving, and the best way to get ahead was to mount a horse and canter him from stage to stage, that is, between twelve and fifteen miles a day.

Invading armies had, of course, made use of the Road long before the British gained control of northern

India. On this same stretch of the highway, the Persian invader Nadir Shah defeated the Mughal Emperor in 1739. In a battle lasting two hours, over 20,000 of the Emperor's soldiers were killed. The next day Nadir Shah marched to Delhi, to sack the city and massacre its inhabitants. The treasure harvest of Delhi was fair game for acquisitive kings and warlords.

When the British consolidated their power in India, they found the Road, stretching as it did from Calcutta to Peshawar, a great line of communication. Kipling's 'regiment a-marchin' down the GT Road' was a common enough sight throughout the nineteenth century. During the 1857 uprising, after the British were ousted from Delhi, their army assembled at Ambala and came marching down the GT Road to lay siege to the city of Delhi. A few years later a junior officer, recalling the march, wrote:

> The stars were bright in the dark deep sky and the fireflies flashed from bush to bush . . . Along the road came the heavy roll of the guns, mixed with the jangling of bits and the clanking of the scabbards of the cavalry. The infantry marched behind with a deep, dull tread. Camels and bullock carts, with innumerable camp servants,

toiled away for miles in the rear, while gigantic elephants, pulling the heavy guns, came lumbering down the road.

Some thirty years after the 1857 uprising came the Afghan Wars, and the GT Road became an all-important route for the British army proceeding towards Peshawar and the Khyber Pass. Those were the days of military manoeuvres all over north India, and my grandfather, a foot soldier in the mould of Kipling's 'soldiers three', found himself 'route marchin', that is, foot-slogging all over northern and central India. Wives and children followed the regiment wherever it was sent, and military camps and cantonments sprang up everywhere. Children were often born in the course of these marches and troop movements: my father at Shahjahanpur (not far from the Road), his brothers and sisters at places as far apart as Barrackpore, Campbellpur and Dera Ismail Khan!

The tedium of the march was broken only by the sight of fields of golden corn stretching towards the horizon, with mango groves rising like islands from the flat plain; but for the most part it was monotonous tramping, exemplified in this marching song of Kipling's:

> Oh, there's them Indian temples to admire when
>   you see,

> There's the peacock round the corner
> An' the monkey up the tree.
> With our best foot first
> And the Road a-sliding past,
> An' every bloomin' camping-ground
> Exactly like the last.

I can sing this song myself, having listened to Nelson Eddy's rendering of it hundreds of times on the old wind-up gramophone my father carried about with him for years.

Kipling immortalized the Road in *Kim* and *Barrack-Room Ballads* (he had a strong empathy with the common soldier), and but for him, few outside of India would have heard of the Grand Trunk Road. But Kipling would not recognize the Road today. Cars, buses, tractors, trucks, all thunder down the highway, and even the bullock carts are equipped with heavy tyres. It's a very democratic mix. Nowhere else in the world are you likely to find such a variety of traffic, or so many impediments to vehicular progress—cows, cart-horses, buffaloes, cyclists, stray hens, stray villagers, stray policemen.

'Proceed at Your Own Risk.' You could call this the motto of the Road, a motto vividly illustrated by overturned lorries lying in ditches, buses upended against trees or dangling over culverts, fancy cars crushed into concertina shapes, squashed cats and dogs, mangled drivers and passengers. These are common sights, along with the endless panorama of field, factory, village or township.

For the towns and cities grow bigger by the day. They spread octopus-like over the rural landscape, and the traffic spills out in an endless, honking procession of humankind on wheels. 'OK Tata,' proclaims the truck in front of you, and it would be wise to keep your distance. What's your choice of vehicle for making progress on the Road? Motorcycle, taxi, limousine, or buffalo cart? Mine's a steamroller. No one pushes it around.

I have never travelled the entire length of the Road, but I have driven along stretches of it. The most memorable one was with Gurbachan Singh.

As his taxi weaved its way in and out of the Amritsar traffic, and headed for Delhi, Gurbachan Singh took his hand off the horn and gave me a brief triumphant look.

'What do you think of my horn?' he asked.

'Oh, it's a fine horn,' I said, wringing out my ears. 'It couldn't be louder.'

'You can hear it half a mile ahead,' said Gurbachan proudly, as he blasted off at two young men who were sharing a bicycle. They moved out of the way with alacrity.

'It makes a lot of noise in the car, too,' I said, and added hastily, 'not that I object, you know . . .'

'Doesn't your horn have more than one tone of voice?' asked a fellow traveller with a trace of irritation.

'Two!' claimed Gurbachan. 'Male and female. Just see!' And he produced a high note and then a low note on the horn, both equally ear-shattering. Ahead of us, a tonga ran off the road and on to the cart track.

'This is one terrific horn,' said Gurbachan. 'I have had it made especially for this taxi. No foreign horns for me. They are not loud enough. Indian horns are best.'

'Indian noise is best,' said the fellow traveller.

In an interval of comparative quiet, I found myself reflecting on the nature of sound—the unpleasantness of some sounds, and the sweetness of others, and why certain sounds (like motor horns) can be sweet to some and hideous to others. The sweetest sound of all, I decided, was silence. There are many kinds of silence—the silence of an empty room, the silence of the mountains, the silence of prayer, or the enforced silence of loneliness—but the best kind of silence, I concluded, was the silence that comes after the cessation of noise.

'It was made in the Jama Masjid area,' continued Gurbachan, interrupting my thoughts. 'Seventy-five rupees only. Made by hand, to my own specification. There's only one drawback: it must not get wet!'

As his hand settled down on the horn again, I thought of praying for rain, but the sky being clear and blue, I decided that a prayer would be an unreasonable demand on the Creator.

'Ah, but you don't know what it is to have a horn like this one. Try it, sir. Why don't you try it for yourself?'

'Oh, that's all right,' I assured him. 'You have proved its excellence already.'

'No, you must try it. I insist that you try it!' He was like a big boy, suddenly generous, determined on sharing a new toy with a younger brother.

He grabbed my hand and placed it on the horn; and, as I felt it give a little, a thrill of pleasure rushed up my arm. I pressed hard, and a stream of music flowed in and out of the car. Now I could understand the happiness and the supreme self-confidence of Gurbachan and all drivers like him; for, with a horn like his, one felt the power and glory that belongs to the kings of the Road.

For the rest of the journey Gurbachan drove and I blew the horn.

The fellow passenger, no doubt realizing that he was locked into a taxi with two lunatics, was too terrified to say a word.

~

Spent a week in Dehra, at the old White House Hotel. Dehra is a bit seedy now, but familiar corners bring back memories of childhood and boyhood days. Dear old Dehra: I may stop loving you, but I won't stop loving the days I loved you.

DECEMBER

In today's mail, instead of the Christmas letters I was hoping for a solitary letter, from a certain Evergreen Publications:

> Dear Sir
> Your address has been collected from Children's Book Trust. We are at lost end to know your profession. We are Children Book publishers and we are looking for Artist, Author, Editor. Kindly send your Biodata.

Well, I always thought I was an author by profession, and my tax return says as much. But now I, too, am at a 'lost end'.

~

When I look down from the heights of Landour to the broad valley of the Doon far below, I can see the little Suswa river, silver in the setting sun, meandering through the fields and forests on its way to its confluence with the mighty Ganga.

The Suswa is a river I knew well as a boy, but it has been many years since I swam in its quiet pools or slept in the shade of the tall spreading trees growing on its banks. Now I see it from my window, far away, dreamlike, and I keep promising myself that I will visit it again, to touch its waters, cool and clear, and feel its rounded pebbles beneath my feet.

It's a little river, flowing down from the ancient Siwaliks (which are older than the Himalayas, according to some geologists), running the length of the valley until, with its sister river the Song, it slips into the Ganga just above the holy city of Hardwar. I could wade across it (except during the monsoons, when it was in spate) and the water seldom rose above the waist except in sheltered pools, where it was chin-deep and where I swam gently through shoals of small fish.

There is a little-known legend about the Suswa and its origins, which I have always treasured. It tells us that the Hindu sage, Kasyapa, once gave a great feast to which all the gods were invited. Now Indra, the god of rain, while on his way to the entertainment, happened to meet 60,000 *balkhils* (pygmies) of the Brahmin caste, who were trying in vain to cross a cow's footprint filled with water, to them a vast lake.

The god could not restrain his laughter and scoffed at them. The indignant priests, determined to have their revenge, at once set to work creating a second Indra, who should supplant the reigning god. This could only be done by means of penance and mortification, in which they persevered, until the sweat flowing from their tiny bodies made the river known as the 'Suswa', or 'flowing waters'.

Indra, alarmed at the effect of these religious exercises, sought the intercession of Brahma, the Creator, through whose good offices he was able to keep his position as the rain god.

I saw no pygmies or fairies near the Suswa, but once, lying full length on its grassy verge, I looked up to see, on the opposite bank, a magnificent tiger drinking at the water's edge. It was only some sixty feet away, and I lay very still and watched it until it too raised its head, sniffed the wind (which fortunately blew towards me) and then walked regally downstream and out of sight.

I do not remember feeling afraid. As children we do not have a fear of wild animals unless it is inculcated in us. And animals are quick to sense fear in a human. But I am unable to test my reactions as an adult for, alas, there are no longer any tigers in the forests near the Suswa.

Still, I must go down to that river again, to its gently flowing waters but only after the monsoons, when Indra the rain god has reasserted himself.

~

In every small town or cantonment of India, there is, or used to be, an English cemetery. These graves, some of them going back to the seventeenth century, are perhaps the most eloquent memorials to the British presence in India. Soldiers and civilians, women and children, many of them cut down in their prime by diseases for which there were then no cures, lie here in their thousands, mute testimony to the hazards of empire building.

Many old cemeteries lie in ruins; some have disappeared altogether. Their disappearance is perhaps inevitable in a land where the pressures of an ever-increasing urban population result in the view that an old cemetery is really an ideal building site. Some of them, like the Camel's Back and Landour cemeteries in Mussoorie, are beauty spots in themselves, the trees still standing (even thriving, thanks to those good old bones), and usually facing north, with views of the eternal snows. Men come and go and even nations die, but the mountains remain . . .

What brought Mr Alfred Hindmarsh to Mussoorie? The inscription tells us that he was 'One of the six hundred' and there were not many of them left after the Charge of the Light Brigade in 1854. In the Crimean War, at Balaclava, a command was misinterpreted and the flower of the British cavalry charged across the 'valley of death' upon the Russian guns, to their inevitable destruction. Only a hundred rode back to their lines.

> Cannon to right of them,
> Cannon to left of them,
> Cannon behind them
> Volley'd and thunder'd;
> Storm'd at with shot and shell,
> While horse and hero fell,
> They that had fought so well
> Came thro' the jaws of Death,

Back from the mouth of Hell,
All that was left of them,
Left of six hundred.

Hindmarsh was one of those immortalized in Tennyson's lines. Later he must have been sent to India with his regiment, finally retiring in the peace and quiet of Mussoorie. His wife lies beside him.

Frederick Wilson's wife also lies besides him. Wilson—'Pahari Wilson' as he came to be called—was an adventurer who turned up in the hills of Tehri Garhwal in the 1860s. He made a fortune in timber, being the first man to float logs down the Ganga. After marrying a village girl, Gulabi, he settled down to the good life in Mussoorie. Hunting elephants, horses, carriages, fine houses in several beauty spots ... these were only some of Wilson's many assets.

Perhaps his most spectacular achievement was the building of a 350-feet suspension bridge over the Jad Ganga at Bhairoghat. It connected two rocky promontories over the turbulent Bhagirathi. We are told (in Andrew Wilson's *Abode of Snow*) that because of its dizzy height and ultra-vision span, this bridge proved a source of terror to travellers and only a daring few ventured across the rippling contraption. To reassure people,

Wilson assembled a host of Brahmins who kindled a scared fire and chanted hymns. On this auspicious occasion five score goats were slaughtered in sacrifice. But even then, the bridge was not for the faint-hearted. So Wilson mounted his half-Arab grey and galloped it to and fro across the bridge.

Another man who made a fortune and who lies buried here, was John Lang, the first Australian-born novelist, who spent his last years in Mussoorie. The novels of his Indian period have been unjustly neglected (he painted a very satirical picture of British social life), but some of his early Australian work—*The Forger's Wife*, *Botany Bay*—is enjoying a revival.

Lang was a man of many parts. He was a barrister-at-law, who represented the Rani of Jhansi in her legal battle with the East India Company, in the years before the Mutiny. He was handsomely rewarded for his services to the Rani. He also published several newspapers, among them the *Mofussilite* (Meerut), then northern India's premier newspaper. In 1859, two years after the Mutiny, he retired to Mussoorie and died here in 1864. An obituary in the *Mofussilite* told of an incident when Lang lay dying. A public ball had been planned in an apartment of his very large house in Landour and he was asked if the music would disturb him. His immediate and characteristic reply was: 'God forbid that any human enjoyment should be put to a stop on my account.'

Lang had been an anti-establishment figure all his life and had been forced to leave Australia as a young man because of his clashes with the establishment in Sydney. He could not have been very popular with the British diehards either, and his obituary in the conservative *Madras Times* described him as a man who had wasted his talents in dissipation and in acquiring 'the worst of habits'—we are not told what it was!

One of the most handsome mausoleums in the Camel's Back cemetery is that of George Logan (1809-54), an assistant in the Trigonometrical Survey. He came from a prominent Edinburgh family and there were several Logans, indigo planters, in Bengal in the 1830s and '40s. A note in the Survey records (kindly given to me by Colonel Dalal, former Surveyor-General) describes Logan as 'quite the best of Everest's civilian staff, is fully equal to the military officers in general ability and reliability; held charge of trig. parties till death from dysentery after long illness.'

But a humble tombstone can sometimes tell a more dramatic story. For instance, 'Here lies Mr Reginald John Clapp, killed by the hand of one he befriended.' That was in 1909.

Clapp was a chemist's assistant, a popular young man with many friends among the soldiers at the Landour convalescent depot. One of them had cut Clapp's throat and made off with his money. The next day Corporal Allen was arrested. He protested his innocence, and showed no distress when confronted with the body. But he was tried and found guilty and hanged at Bareilly.

Another victim who lies here is Mrs Owen, whose husband went berserk, shooting her and their daughter in a Mussoorie boarding house. The daughter survived. Mr Owen then took his own life. His was the first European cremation in Mussoorie. That was in 1927.

In today's world, cremations are gaining in popularity over burials. They are less expensive, for one thing. Indeed, when one looks at some of the ornate and beautifully sculpted figures and motifs on some of the monuments, one has to concede that such workmanship and material would cost a fortune today. Much of this fine work was done in Meerut and Lucknow, by Hindu and Muslim artisans.

A cemetery is a piece of history and many of the older ones deserve preservation. They have a certain character and charm and they tell us a great deal about ordinary people. They are also permanent reminders of our own impermanence.

JANUARY

The hillside looked very pretty, with a light mantle of snow covering trees, rusty roofs and vehicles at the bus stop, and concealing our garbage dump for a couple of hours, until the snow melted.

~

Three days of wind, rain, sleet and snow. Flooded out of my bedroom. We convert the dining room into dormitory. Everything is bearable except the wind, which cuts through these old houses like a knife under the roof, through flimsy veranda enclosures and ill-fitting windows, bringing the icy rain with it.

~

Fed up with being stuck indoors. Walked up to Lal Tibba, in flurries of snow. Came back and wrote a story.

~

There are some lovely old houses in the Landour cantonment but, sadly, the majority of them lie empty for most of the year. Their owners, the famous and the wealthy, live elsewhere and visit Mussoorie or Landour about once a year, for a weekend's relaxation. It's everyone's dream to own a house in Landour. But once a property has been bought and done up nicely, it's usually forgotten.

A different situation prevails in the 'civil' station of Mussoorie. There we have an acute shortage of accommodation for local residents, not helped by a complete ban on any sort of building, be it hostel or private residence. As a result, the economy is stagnating. In Landour, there is no economy to speak of. The only people with substantial bank deposits are the handful of NGOs who operate from this area.

From November to March you can take a walk up to Lal Tibba or around the Landour *chakkar* without meeting a soul, except for a milkman whose home is down in the valley, or a chowkidar from one of the empty houses, or maybe, if you're lucky, Professor Uniyal, the only year-round resident at the top of the hill. More often than not, he's enjoying the privacy of his garden, tending his wayward nasturtiums and antirrhinums.

One wanders on, past Victor Banerjee's pretty gingerbread house, Prannoy Roy's rock fortress, Tom Alter's rambling family estate, and the stately homes owned by absent Lals, Kapoors, Misras and others, in the hope of stumbling upon some intellectual company. But alas, there is no one in residence—all, all are gone, the old familiar faces! If you're lucky, you might get a glimpse of them next summer, but even that is doubtful.

So it's down the mountain path, in the hope of finding Ganesh Saili at home. But he's in Delhi, picking up an award for encouraging tourism. Where are our other distinguished travel writers? The Gantzers are in Goa, encouraging tourism there. Bill Aitken has gone south and will return only when the wild ducks fly north. Sudhir Thapliyal is entertaining the Press Club in Delhi.

Disconsolately, one turns homewards, passing a honeymoon couple hurrying back to their cold hotel room. They are wishing they'd gone to Chutmalpur instead of a deserted hill station in mid-winter.

Ah! Here's Brigadier Yadav—always good for a tale or two of his days as ADC to Mountbatten. His enthusiasm never flags. But the good Brigadier looks gloomy today. 'I've had enough of this place,' he complains. 'Not a soul to talk to. And I can't take the cold any more. Thinking of moving down to Rajpur.'

One more empty house!

There's one last hope of finding a little company—the cemetery! Those rows of old, weather-worn graves tell of livelier times, when officers and gentlemen tossed back their rum punches and whisky pegs, no doubt hastening their jouney to their final abode. But confound my luck, the cemetery gates are locked and chained, barred to prowlers like me. Now even conversing with the dead is denied.

Never mind, there's always Lakshmi Tripathi's chowkidar. Not much by way of intellectual stimulation, but the hooch isn't bad. He may not be encouraging tourism, but at least he helps the locals get through the lean days.

FEBRUARY

Rummaging through a box of old papers and manuscripts, I came across my address book for the year 1964. I opened it with some trepidation. Almost forty years had passed, and inevitably many of those listed would have passed on—some, perhaps to a better world than this one, or simply to a good long rest . . .

I thought of throwing away the notebook, but curiosity and a respect for the past and all it stood for, made me desist. We are, after all, the products of history, creatures of our own pasts. I opened the address book at random. And had a pleasant surprise. Some of my old friends were still around!

For here was Narinder's address—not the Dilaram Bazaar house where I had known him as a boy, but his

London address, shortly after he had arrived there as a young man in his mid-twenties. A happy ending too, because Narinder (BA third division) went on to run a flourishing wine-importing business in the UK and was a rich man within ten years of starting out. He keeps in touch, and comes to see me occasionally, but he has never sent or brought us a bottle of vintage French wine, or any other wine for that matter. As he doesn't drink the stuff himself, I'm not surprised he's been so successful. If I had a wine business, I'd be tasting the better wines pretty often just to make sure there was no decline in standards!

And here's Hetty Prim's address in Palampur. Hetty was a teacher who wrote children's stories on the side. I remember her with gratitude and affection because she taught me to cook at a time when I was living on my own, surviving on boiled eggs and bread and butter. Towards the end of this same notebook I had recorded some of the recipes I had tried out, quite successfully, and reproduce two or three here for the benefit of bachelors in similar situations:

Soup a la Hetty
   3 tomatoes
   ½ cabbage
   small piece ginger, cut fine

1 onion

3 teaspoons salt

2 or 3 tablespoons ghee

Cook in *degchi* three-quarters full of water for ½ hour. For thickening, add 2 spoons atta in ½ cup milk. Serve with pepper. Voila!

Alu Bhuji

Boil 8 small potatoes. Peel and cut into slices. Fry an onion in ghee, add pinch of haldi, potatoes, 1 teaspoon salt, ½ teaspoon red chilli powder, 1 tomato (optional), 2 green chillies (optional).

Stir on slow fire till mashed. (Do not add water.)

Dal

Malka (pink) dal. One teacup full to be cleaned and washed and boiled.

Fry onion in ghee till brown but not burnt. Keep aside one teaspoon haldi, 1 teaspoon red chilli. ½ teaspoon salt.

Add to browned onions and immediately add ¼ cup water.

My pink Malka dal became all the rage on the hillside! (If you forget haldi, it stays pink, otherwise it turns yellow.)

There are several others but I shall keep them for

that cookbook I plan to write some day! I should add that all my dishes ware cooked in ordinary degchis and not in pressure cookers which made me nervous.

A belated thanks to Hetty for helping to see me through those lean years. I believe she still lives in Palampur, where she settled with her family many years ago.

~

Thomas Hardy was once a guest at a literary dinner where the conversation centred around the pronunciation of certain words. A member of the company turned towards Hardy and said, 'Have you ever noticed that in the entire English language there is only one word beginning with "su" that is pronounced as though beginning with "sh".'

'Really,' said Hardy. 'And what is the word?'
'Sugar.'

The novelist assumed an expression of interest and quietly remarked, 'Are you sure?'

~

'Stand still for ten minutes, and they'll build a hotel on top of you,' said one old-timer to me today, gesturing towards the concrete jungle that had sprung up along Mussoorie's Mall, the traditional promenade.

And indeed as I looked, it seemed one long, ugly bazaar, though if you leave the Mall and walk along some of the old lanes and by-ways, you will come across many old houses, most of them still bearing the names they were given in the mid-nineteenth century.

Mussoorie, like other hill resorts in India, came into existence in the 1820s or thereabouts, when the families of British colonials began making for the hills in order to escape the scorching heat of the plains. Small settlements grew into large 'stations', and were soon vying with each other for the title of 'Queen of the Hills'. Mussoorie's name derives from the Mansur shrub (*Cororiana nepalensis*), common in the Himalayan foothills; but many of the house names derive from the native places of those who first built and lived in them. Today, though these houses and estates are owned by well-to-do Indians, in most cases the old names have been retained.

Take for instance, the 'Mullingar'. This is not one of the better preserved buildings, having been under litigation for some years; but it was a fine mansion once, and it has the distinction of being the oldest building in Mussoorie. It was the home, naturally enough, of an Irishman, Captain Young, who commanded the first

Gurkha battalion when it was in its infancy. As you have probably guessed, he came from Mullingar, in old Ireland, and it was to Ireland that he finally returned, when he gave up his sword and saddle. There is a story that on moonlit nights a ghostly rider can be seen on the Mullingar flat, and that this is Captain Young revisiting old haunts.

There must have been a number of Irishmen settling and building in Mussoorie in those pioneering days, for there are houses with names such as 'Tipperary', 'Killarney' and 'Shamrock'. 'The harp that once in Tara's Halls' must have sounded in Shimla too, for there is also a Tara Hall in the old summer capital of India.

As everywhere else, the Scots were great pioneers in Mussoorie, and were quick to identify Himalayan hills and meadows with their own glens and braes. There are over a dozen house names prefixed with 'Glen', and close to where I live there is a 'Scotsburn', a 'Wolfsburn', and a 'Redburn'. A burn is a small stream, but there are none in the vicinity, so the names must have been given for purely sentimental reasons.

The English, of course, went in for castles—there's 'Connaught Castle' and 'Grey Castle' and 'The Castle Hill', the latter home for a time to the exiled young Sikh prince, Dalip Singh, before he went to England to become a protégé of Queen Victoria.

Sir Walter Scott must have been a very popular writer with the British in exile, for there are many houses in Mussoorie that were named after his novels and romances: 'Kenilworth', 'Ivanhoe', 'Waverley', 'Rokeby' and 'The Monastery'. And there is also 'Abbotsford', named after Scott's own home.

Dickens' lovers must have felt frustrated, because they could hardly name their houses 'Nicholas Nickleby' or 'Martin Chuzzlewit'; but one Dickens fan did come up with 'Bleak House' for a name, and bleak it is, even to this day. I have never had the money to buy or build a house of my own, but I am ever the optimist, and if ever I do have one, I shall call it 'Great Expectations'.

Mussoorie did have a Dickens connection. In 1850, when Charles Dickens was publishing his magazine *Household Words*, his correspondent in India was John Lang, who lies buried in the Camel's Back cemetery. His diverting account of a typical Mussoorie 'season', called 'The Himalaya Club', appeared in *Household Words* in the issue of 21 March 1857.

I haven't been able to locate the house in which Lang lived, but from one of his descriptions it may have been 'White Park Forest', now practically a ruin. The name is another puzzle, because of park or forest there is no trace. But on looking up an old guide, I discovered that it had been named after its joint owners, Mr White, Mr Park and Mr Forest.

Another name that puzzled me for a time was that of the old Charleville Hotel, now an academy for young civil servants. Was it French in its origins? Most of the locals always referred to it as the 'Charley-Billy' Hotel, which I thought was an obvious mispronunciation; but the laugh was really on me. According to the records, the original owner had two sons, Charley and Billy, and he had named the hotel after them!

This naming of places is never as simple as it may seem. Mossy Falls is a small waterfall on the outskirts of the town. You might think it was named after the moss that is so plentiful around it, but you'd be wrong. It was really named after Mr Moss, the owner of the Alliance Bank who was affectionately known as Mossy to his friends. When, at the turn of the century, the Alliance Bank collapsed, Mr Moss also fell from grace. 'Poor old Mossy,' said his friends, and promptly named the falls after him.

MARCH

It is now twenty years since *Room on the Roof* was first reprinted in an edition meant for schools. This was when my work first became familiar to schoolchildren throughout the country. And of course that was twenty years after the book had been published originally, and during those years it was to all practical purposes forgotten!

Although I did not set out to be a children's writer, some of my early stories did appear in children's magazines, such as *Young Elizabethan*. My first children's book (written specifically for children) was *Angry River*, published by Hamish Hamilton in 1972. After that, there was one every year published by Hamish Hamilton and then by Julia MacRae. Sadly, in the early 1990s, Julia Machae was swallowed up by a multinational and most of my titles disappeared; but I was able to reissue them in India. Now, when I'm asked if I write for adults or for children, I can honestly say that I write for myself.

~

Holi brings warmer days, ladybirds, new friends. Trees in new leaf. The fresh light green of the maples is very soothing.

I may not have contributed anything towards the progress of civilization, but neither have I robbed the world of anything. Not one tree or bush or bird or flower. Even the spider on my wall is welcome to his (her) space.

~

Blizzard in the night. Over a foot of snow in the morning. And so it goes on ... unprecedented for March. The Jupiter effect? At least the snow prevents the roof from blowing away, as happened one year. Facing east (from where the wind blows) doesn't help. And it's such a rickety old house.

~

During my adult life I have been doing my best to see a ghost, or even feel the presence of a ghostly being; but, apart from hearing about other people's hair-raising experiences, I have never had any supernatural visitations.

So when Roop Singh told me that his wife (who had recently arrived from their village in the mountain fastnesses near Gangotri) was possessed by a ghost or evil spirit, I was delighted. Here, at last, was my chance to experience the real thing.

Our adventure took place in the middle of a stormy night last month. It was raining heavily, but I am a light sleeper, and at about one in the morning I was awakened by Roop Singh calling, 'Sir, sir! Please come!'

I found his wife making strange, mewling sounds, as she moved restlessly around the room, shifting rapidly between door and window. Her hair was loose and there was a wild look in her staring eyes. She seemed totally unaware of my presence.

'The spirit is calling her outside,' said Roop Singh, and whacked her over the head with the flat of his hand. 'That's the only thing that brings her to her senses,' he explained.

The girl, now awake, sank down on the cot, sobbing hysterically. 'She's all right now,' said Roop Singh. 'But the spirit will return later, and then she'll be up and about again.'

'Let's wait and see what happens,' I said

Soon she began to whimper again. The whimper became a muttering. And then she was talking to someone, and it was quite clear that she wasn't talking to either Roop Singh or me.

As Roop Singh raised his heavy hand once more, I said, 'Wait! Hold it!' And dashing upstairs in the rain, I found a little bottle of smelling salt, last opened some ten years ago.

I held the bottle close to the girl's quivering nostrils. Her head jerked back, and she was instantly awake.

'Here, you keep it,' I said, presenting the bottle to Roop Singh. 'Whenever the ghost visits her, be sure to use it!'

He's done this ever since, and claims my cure is infallible. But he doesn't accept my theory that his wife is simply a sleepwalker and a sleep talker. 'We call it a ghost,' he says.

And he may be right. But if ghosts are susceptible to smelling salts, then once again I am disillusioned. I lost my respect for vampires many years ago, when I learnt that they fled from the smell of garlic. And now I find that ghosts are equally chicken-hearted. There's no integrity left in the spirit world. Humans are far more frightening.

~

Mid-March and the first warm breath of approaching summer. Peach, plum and apricot trees in blossom. School reopens. Siddharth and Shrishti are resplendent in bright new uniforms; Gautam insists on having one too, although he hasn't started school as yet.

Sold German and Dutch translation rights in a couple of my children's books. I wish I could write something of lasting worth. I've done a few good stories but they are so easily buried in the mass of literature that pours forth from the world's presses.

Risk a haircut. Ramkumar does his best to make me look like a 1930s film star. I suppose I ought to try another barber, but he's too nice.

'I look rather strange,' I said afterwards.

'Don't worry,' he said. 'You'll get used to it.'

I might, but Nandu and Ganesh had a good laugh. 'You look like one of the Three Stooges,' said Nandu. 'And you're the other two,' I snapped.

~

The 'adventure wind' of my boyhood I felt it again today. Walked five miles to Suakholi, to look at an infinity of mountains. The feeling of space—limitless space—can only be experienced by living in the mountains.

It is the emotional, the spiritual surge, that draws us back to the mountains again and again. It was not altogether a matter of mysticism or religion that prompted the ancients to believe that their gods dwelt in the high places of this earth. Those gods, by whatever name we know them, still dwell there. From time to time we would like to be near them, that we may know them and ourselves more intimately.

~

Late March.

The blackest cloud I've ever seen squatted over Mussoorie, and then it hailed marbles for half an hour. Nothing like a hailstorm to clear the sky. Even as I write, I see a rainbow forming. Gautam is excited by it—his first rainbow—and repeats the colours as I name them. Has a little difficulty with indigo.

~

Can thought (consciousness) exist outside the body? Can it be trained to do so? Can its existence continue after the body has gone? Does it need a body? (But without a body it would have nothing to do.)

Of course thoughts can travel. But do they travel of their own volition, or because of the bodily energy that sustains them?

We have the wonders of clairvoyance, of presentiments and premonitions in dreams. How to account for these?

Our thinking is conditioned by past experience (including the past experience of the human race), and so, as Bergson said: 'We think with only a small part of the past, but it is with our entire past, including the original bent of the soul, that we desire, will and act.'

'The original bent of the soul . . .' I accept that man has a soul, or he would be incapable of compassion.

~

Some Night Thoughts (Written after one of my nocturnal walks)

    The mountain is my mother,
    My father is the sea,
    This river is the fountain

Of all that life can be.
Swift river from the mountain,
Deep river to the sea,
Take all my words and leave them
Where the trade winds set them free.
Oh, piper on the lonely hill,
Play no sad songs for me.
The day has gone, the night comes on,
Its darkness helps me see.